THE
TOUCH
OF
MAGIC

Books by Lorena A. Hickok

STORY OF ELEANOR ROOSEVELT

STORY OF FRANKLIN D. ROOSEVELT

STORY OF HELEN KELLER

LADIES OF COURAGE (*with Eleanor Roosevelt*)

Helen Keller, left, and Anne Sullivan Macy on the lawn
at the summer home of Dr. Alexander Graham Bell

THE
TOUCH
OF
MAGIC

THE STORY OF
HELEN KELLER'S GREAT TEACHER
ANNE SULLIVAN MACY

BY

LORENA A. HICKOK

DODD, MEAD & COMPANY
NEW YORK
1961

To the best teacher I ever had,
Miss Alicent Holt,
who taught me Latin, Greek and manners
in Battle Creek, Michigan, High School
many years ago

Grateful acknowledgment is made for permission to quote from the following:

Anne Sullivan Macy by Nella Braddy. Copyright 1933 by Nella Braddy Henney. Reprinted by permission of Doubleday & Co., Inc.
Letter of Carl Sandburg to Helen Keller, April 8, 1922.
The Portable Woollcott, selected by Joseph P. Hennessey. "In Memoriam: Annie Sullivan" by Alexander Woollcott. Published by The Viking Press, Inc.
The Story of My Life by Helen Keller. Copyright 1902, 1903, 1905 by Helen Keller. Reprinted by permission of Doubleday & Co., Inc.
Teacher by Helen Keller. Copyright © 1955 by Helen Keller. Reprinted by permission of Doubleday & Company, Inc.

FOREWORD

MOST AUTHORS will tell you that writing a book is a lonely business. It is. But very few books—if any—fiction or non-fiction, were ever written whose authors did not receive help from someone.

First, there is the research, interviews, reading and studying the work of other writers, manuscripts, letters. In this case, the interview was with Helen Keller and the late Polly Thomson. The writer was then working on a book for children about Miss Keller, but Teacher, as they affectionately called her, inevitably came into the conversation. She always did.

Reading research for this book consisted of: Nella Braddy's comprehensive and fascinating biography of Anne Sullivan Macy, published some thirty years ago; Helen Keller's *Story of My Life,* containing her childhood letters and the invaluable letters her teacher wrote during the months after she had released little Helen from her dark and silent prison; Helen Keller's beautiful and inspiring book, *Teacher—Anne Sullivan Macy;* Alexander Woollcott's moving tribute to Annie Sullivan, which appeared in

v

the *Atlantic Monthly* after her death; and the files of *The New York Times*. The author is very grateful to publishers and writers of letters for some of the material in this book—especially to Carl Sandburg for permission to quote from a letter he once wrote to Miss Keller.

And there are people who help. Nannine Joseph, so much more than a literary agent, but a dear and devoted friend. Mr. Allen Klots, Jr., a superb editor, who helped this writer in ways far beyond what any author should expect from an editor. Jean Taylor Hartwig, who volunteered to copy the manuscript for nothing. The staff of the Franklin D. Roosevelt Library, at Hyde Park, who dug out the stories from the files of *The New York Times* and found Alexander Woollcott's article.

And finally there was Annie Sullivan herself. No author ever finished a book with greater regret. During the months I worked on this book she became as real to me as a living person—a warm, very human, greatly loved friend. I miss her. Not as Miss Keller must miss her always. But nevertheless I miss her.

LORENA A. HICKOK

CONTENTS

✕

CHAPTER I

THE UNWANTED

THE DAY was Washington's Birthday. The year, 1876. Through the cold February twilight, an ugly black conveyance jolted and rattled on high iron-rimmed wheels over a frozen dirt road through the outskirts of Tewksbury, Massachusetts.

It had only one small window, covered with iron bars, in the padlocked rear door. Along the sides, up near the top, were narrow slits, presumably to let in a little light and air. It was drawn by two dejected-looking horses.

Housewives, cleaning up after their children's Washington's Birthday parties, frowned as they glanced out their windows and saw it go by. For it was called "the Black Maria," and it was used to haul criminals off to jail.

The passengers on this trip, however, were not under arrest. There were two of them, a small boy and girl huddled together on one of the long wooden benches that ran along the sides. The Black Maria was borrowed to take people to the place where they were going. It belonged to the town, and it was the only conveyance available.

The bench was worn and slippery, and the children

clung desperately to each other to keep from falling off. The boy had a crutch, and he whimpered and sometimes cried out in pain as the cumbersome vehicle swayed and lurched in the frozen ruts.

Outside the town, the Black Maria turned into a driveway, passed through a big gate and stopped in front of a large building that looked run-down and rickety even in the dim wintry dusk. A man who had brought them out from Boston on a train climbed down from the front seat, where he had ridden with the driver, and led the tired, half-frozen passengers up some creaking steps, across a sagging porch and into a big hall dimly lighted with kerosene lamps. Nine-year-old Annie Sullivan and her little brother Jimmie had arrived at their new home.

It was called the Massachusetts State Infirmary. But there were no nurses about, in starched white uniforms. When doctors came there—and they seldom came unless called in an emergency—they received no pay. Although its name implied that it was a hospital, this was actually the state almshouse, grudgingly supported by the legislature at a cost of $1.88 per week for each patient.

The patients were people whom nobody wanted around. Some were insane; some were alcoholics. Some were foundlings, born out of wedlock. Most of the babies did not live long, for there was not enough money to give them proper food and care. Many of the inmates were old people, no longer able to work, without money and with nobody to support them. Here they were sent to die, out of sight and forgotten. In their misery, some of them welcomed death as a release.

Annie and Jimmie were sent there because they had no other place to go. Their mother was dead, and their father had deserted them. Annie's eyes were bad, and Jimmie had a lump on his hip which the doctor said was tuberculous. He was unable to walk without a crutch. Nobody wanted a nine-year-old girl who was going blind or a little boy who was a cripple.

The trouble with Annie's eyes had started before she was three years old. They became badly inflamed as little lumps began to form on the insides of her eyelids. The disease was trachoma, which is most apt to occur where sanitary conditions are bad. It is a virus that can be carried by flies, and window screens were a luxury beyond the means of families situated as the Sullivans were. When a person has trachoma, the lumps inside the eyelids, soft and fuzzy at first, eventually become hard, like calluses. These keep scratching the eyeballs, causing ulcers and scar tissue. Gradually the scar tissue covers the eyes, and blindness results.

With proper care and treatment in the beginning, Annie's sight might have been saved. But her father, working as a day laborer on farms around Feeding Hills, Massachusetts, where Annie was born, spent most of his meager pay on cheap whisky. There was little enough left to buy food, let alone to pay doctor bills. Her mother, crippled and ill herself, did not know what was wrong with Annie's eyes. A neighbor woman told her to wash them with "geranium water." So she would pluck leaves off a scrawny plant that somehow managed to survive in a tin can on her kitchen window. These she cooked up into a brew that smarted and made Annie howl with pain when it was applied to her sore, inflamed eyes. It did no good. Annie's father, who would sometimes be in an amiable mood when he came home drunk on pay day, said her eyes could be cured with drops of water from the River Shannon. But Feeding Hills was a long, long way from Ireland and the River Shannon.

Annie was not quite nine and Jimmie three when their

mother died of tuberculosis. Of the three little Sullivans left motherless, only one was healthy and attractive. Mary, less than a year old, was a sweet, cuddly baby, and she was promptly adopted by relatives. They took Jimmie, too, but unwillingly and on a temporary basis.

For several months, Annie lived on with her father in a wretched, tumble-down cabin. While the memory of her mother's death was still fresh, the neighbors frequently sent in left-over dishes, and now and then one of the women would come in and help Annie clean house. But the neighbors had many mouths to feed, money was scarce and the women were busy looking after their own families. A child, nearly blind, trying to keep house for a father who came home on pay day drunk and with empty pockets, was in a hopeless situation. Finally her father did not come home at all, and the Sullivan relatives had to get together and decide what to do about Annie.

Annie, just turning nine, was strong, well developed and healthy, except for her eyes. She had thick, soft brown hair, a lovely Irish complexion and beautifully curved lips that gave her face, in repose, a wistful expression. But her blue eyes were scarred and cloudy, the lids red and inflamed. All through her girlhood, people would say of her, "She'd be pretty if it weren't for her eyes."

Finding a home for Annie would have been difficult enough because she was going blind. She also had a very bad disposition, was subject to violent outbursts of temper and had never in her short life shown the slightest trace of love or affection for anyone. A child psychologist would have understood that a child in her predicament would be apt to develop into a little lone wolf fighting the world. But her Sullivan relatives knew nothing of child psychology. She was simply not a nice little girl, and nobody wanted her.

She was finally taken into the home of her father's cousin John, the most prosperous of the Sullivans. John and his wife, Anastatia, whom the relatives called "Statia," did not want her, but since they were better off than the others, they could not very well get out of it. John was a tobacco farmer, and he and Statia lived in a big white house, the cleanest, most comfortable house Annie had ever seen. They had several children, and Statia may have consoled herself with the thought that at least Annie could earn her keep by helping with the housework. If she had any such hope, however, she was soon disillusioned. Annie could not see well enough to do much, and she was so rude and at times so violent that Statia was a little afraid of her. Before long, Annie was left pretty much to her own devices, so long as she did not break anything in one of her tantrums. When autumn came, the other children went to school. Annie wanted to go, too, but when she asked Statia about it she was told harshly, "Don't be a fool. With your eyes, you could never learn to read or write." So Annie wandered out to the big red tobacco sheds to play by herself.

"She's a queer one," John remarked. "She can't get along with people, but with animals and birds she gets along fine. This afternoon she was lying out there on the ground, so quiet that sparrows were hopping all around her, even lighting on her hands. They weren't the least bit afraid of her."

"Well, I am when she starts throwing things," his wife replied. "I don't know what to do with her."

Annie's troubles came to a head on Christmas morning. For several days, packages had been carried into the "front parlor," which was hardly ever used except for weddings and wakes. From the other children, she learned that these were Christmas presents, and that each child, including Annie, would get some on Christmas morning. The children were forbidden to go in there. So, naturally, Annie went.

Several of the packages had been unwrapped, and among them Annie found, to her amazement and delight, a beautiful doll. Even with her bad eyes, she could see that it had golden curls—"Just like real hair!" she told herself in wonder. It wore a lovely blue dress, and it had arms and legs that moved. Almost afraid to touch it, Annie picked it up and cradled it in her arms, crooning to it softly. Never before had she known such ecstasy. This was going to be her Christmas present! It had to be! It was her doll. Nobody could take it away from her. Whenever she had a chance, she would slip into the parlor and hold the doll in her arms.

Early Christmas morning, the parlor doors were opened, and the children trooped in. Cousin John played Santa Claus, and Annie waited tensely as he started distributing the presents. There were two for her, but she dropped them on the floor without looking at them. Frowning because she couldn't see very well, she stared at the doll. Finally Cousin John picked it up—her doll—and smilingly handed it to one of the other children, who squealed with delight as it was placed in her arms.

For an instant Annie stood frozen as the realization dawned on her that her doll had been given to someone else. Then she flew into a rage the like of which even Cousin John and Statia had never seen before. First she tried to grab the doll from her little cousin, but Cousin John seized her roughly and pushed her away. Then she stamped on her own presents and started smashing everything she could reach—toys, Christmas-tree ornaments, a vase which Statia had received as a wedding gift.

"She's just a wild animal," Statia said after they had

finally quieted her down and had cleaned up the debris. "I can't have her around any longer. I won't!"

A few days later, the Sullivans held another family council. Something would have to be done with Annie, and with Jimmie, too. The lump on Jimmie's hip was as big as a teacup. He would never be anything but a sickly little boy, a burden. The children's father was contributing nothing to their support. Most of the time, nobody knew where he was.

There was one place to go for help—the town. When the village authorities were consulted, they said the children were paupers and wards of the state. The place for them was the State Infirmary, at Tewksbury. The Sullivans had no idea what the place was like. Even if they had known, it might not have made any difference. Their one concern was to get rid of two troublesome burdens.

Annie, of course, knew nothing about the family council or the arrangements. She was excited and felt very important that cold February morning when a horse-drawn hack, with Jimmie inside, pulled up in front of Cousin John's house. With Jimmie was a strange man, one of the town officials. The "nice man," the children were told, was going to take them to Springfield, where they would go for a ride on a train. Neither Annie nor Jimmie had ever ridden on a train. Only once had they ridden in a carriage—to their mother's funeral.

Jubilant at the prospect of these treats, Annie could hardly wait while Statia packed her few belongings in a cardboard box. When they were ready to leave, Statia tried to kiss Annie, something she had never done before.

"You might at least try to be a good girl at a time like this!" she said resentfully as Annie jerked herself away. There were no more good-bys, and Annie did not look back as the hack rattled off down the road.

From Springfield they took a train to Boston, where they would change for Tewksbury. At first Annie and Jimmie were delighted with the journey—the elegant red plush seats; the passing landscape outside the windows; the conductor in a uniform with brass buttons who punched their tickets with a little nickel-plated "gun"; the boy selling peanuts, apples, crackerjack and magazines, who, the man said, was a "news butcher." Their companion bought a magazine for himself and some crackerjack for the children.

Long before they reached Boston, however, the novelty of their first train ride had worn off. Watching the scenery go by hurt Annie's eyes and made her feel sick at her stomach. She did not even enjoy the crackerjack—a rare treat to a child who never had candy and who took her annual spring dose of sulphur and molasses with relish because it tasted sweet. Each time the train lurched to a stop and started up with a jerk, Jimmie bounced on the seat and hurt the lump on his hip.

In Boston, the man bought them some milk and sandwiches, but they were too tired and too confused by the noise and the crowds to eat. And Annie was still car-sick. Their second train trip, from Boston to Tewksbury, was no novelty and no fun. They were exhausted and halffrozen after their ride in the Black Maria when they were led into the big dark hall in the state almshouse.

They were told to sit down on a bench and wait. Behind a desk, a man wearing a green eyeshade began to make notes, talking with the man who had brought them there. Annie and Jimmie paid little attention until they heard the man with the green eyeshade say, "We'll put the girl in with the women. The boy will have to go in the men's ward."

Jimmie caught it first: they were going to be separated. He began to cry and frantically clutched Annie's arm.

Then in a flash something happened to Annie, something wild, fierce, desperate. For the first time in her life she knew she loved another human being. She threw her arms around her little brother and held him close, glaring over his head at the men.

"No! No! No! You can't!" she cried, in a voice that was half-scream and half-growl. "He's my brother!"

Alarmed, the man with the green eyeshade jumped up and came over to them. "There, there, don't cry!" he said, clumsily patting Annie's head. "Don't cry! We'll leave you together."

Looking up at the man who had brought them, he said in a whisper, barely moving his lips, "For tonight, at least."

CHAPTER II

JIMMIE

AFTER A SKIMPY SUPPER, which they were too tired to eat, Annie and Jimmie were taken to a small room at one end of the women's ward.

There was a narrow iron bed. They crawled in and seconds later were sound asleep, Annie with a protecting arm around her brother. Nobody tucked them in or offered to hear their prayers, but, since nobody ever had, they would have been bewildered by such attention.

In the room was a small altar. Whenever one of the old women died out in the ward, the body would be wheeled in to lie there until the men came with a pine box, in which it would be carried out to the potter's field. Sometimes, if there was a clergyman available, there would be a brief funeral service. The room was called "the dead house."

Had Annie and Jimmie known about it, they would not have been disturbed. Death was no mystery to them. They were used to it. Their mother had taken a long time dying. She herself and everyone around her knew that she was dying, and the children had watched her finger with satisfaction the shroud in which she was to be buried. Most of her life she had worn rags. In death she would be decently dressed. A neighbor woman had made the shroud for her own eventual use, but Mrs. Sullivan's need was more immediate, so the neighbor gave it to her.

Annie remembered her mother's funeral as an event both exciting and beautiful. In the carriage, she and Jimmie had fought for the best vantage point from which to watch the horses until their father soundly slapped them both. In the church, she could not look at the candles long, for it hurt her eyes, but the soft light through the stained-glass windows was lovely. There had been other deaths in the Sullivan family, a little sister and a baby brother. There had been no funerals for them. Each time their father rode away in a hack alone, holding a small pine box on his knees.

After breakfast the following morning, Annie and Jimmie waited on a bench in the big dark hall a long time while the superintendent decided what to do with them. Because the foundlings in the maternity ward, in another part of the building, never lived very long, there were no other children in the institution. Finally one of the attendants came to them with a girl's apron—for Jimmie. He started to squirm and howl in protest as they tied it on him, but Annie hurriedly quieted him. If they were to remain together, this was the price he must pay.

Annie and Jimmie settled down happily in the women's ward. They were given adjoining beds, and the dead house was their playroom. Nobody paid much attention to them, and, since she was seldom interfered with, Annie had few tantrums. Whenever she did start to get out of hand, an attendant had only to threaten to send Jimmie to the men's ward—a most effective way of teaching her to control her temper.

The old women in the ward were bedridden, most of them badly crippled with arthritis. There was one exception, a tall woman with white hair, who would pace up and down the ward for hours at a time, usually in the night, muttering to herself. The other patients and the attendants could make out only one word of what she was saying. That word was "lost." So they nicknamed her "Lost," and nobody paid any attention to her.

The other old women did not talk much. They were past the stage where gossip interested them, and, anyway, there was little to gossip about in the dreary procession of these, their final days on earth. Some of them murmured prayers, but most of them just lay on their beds, quietly waiting to die. A groan, sometimes only a long, deep sigh, and it was over. Attendants would wheel the bed, its iron wheels creaking over the uneven wooden floor boards, into the dead house. The bed never remained empty very long. Times were bad, and there were many old women with no other place to go.

Annie and Jimmie had no toys, but they never had had any toys, so they did not miss them. One day they found a pile of dusty old magazines—copies of a women's fashion magazine called *Godey's Lady's Book* and *The Police Gazette,* forerunner of some of today's lurid tabloids. They looked them over, but they were not much interested in them until one day, rummaging in a closet that was supposed to be locked, they found a set of instruments stored there by one of the doctors. Handling the sharp knives and scissors gave Annie an idea. She had often watched Cousin John's children playing with paper dolls. The pictures in the magazines—especially the ladies in pretty colored dresses—would make fine paper dolls. Jimmie had to do most of the cutting, however, for Annie couldn't see well enough, and every now and then she would accidentally snip off a head or an arm.

Jimmie did not care much about playing with paper dolls, but Annie had another inspiration. At school her cousins had made paper chains, held together with flour paste. So Annie managed to wheedle a little flour out of the kitchen help, mixed it with water, and she and Jimmie pasted their paper dolls on the walls of the dead house. The attendants were amused and left them there. The game ended abruptly one day when the doctor found them cutting out paper dolls with his instruments.

"You little devils," he said, "if I ever catch you doing this again, I'll cut off your ears!"

Evenings in the women's ward, lighted by only one flickering, smoky kerosene lamp over the door into the dead house, were never dull for Annie and Jimmie. The place was alive with cockroaches and mice, and along the baseboards were some large rat holes. Cockroaches, mice and even big, gray rats held no terror for Annie and Jimmie. They had lived with them most of their lives. Jimmie would make a long paper squill and poke it into the rat holes, shouting with glee when an infuriated rat would leap out and race madly around the ward. The bedridden old women would scream, and an attendant would come running to see what was causing the uproar. Annie and Jimmie would be scolded and sent to bed, but it was almost bedtime anyway. They might have sent Jimmie to the men's ward to punish him, but, if they had, they would have lost a convenient way of controlling Annie.

The days grew longer, the ice and snow melted and spring arrived. On April 14, Annie was ten years old, but nobody took note of it. She did not even know it was her birthday. Since she had never had any birthday presents or a birthday cake, birthdays meant nothing to her. When anyone asked her when her birthday was, she would answer pertly, "The Fourth of July." That was a date to remember because of the fireworks.

As the days grew milder, Annie began to go outdoors to play, riding up and down the driveway in one of the rickety old wheel chairs that were kept on the porch. Sometimes she would talk with the old men who came out to sit on the benches in the sun. They were not so quiet or so resigned as the old women were. They blamed their plight on "the government," and "the government" was a man named Grant. Annie had never heard of the Civil War or of General U. S. Grant. She did not know he was President. But he was "the government," and she thought he must be a very bad man.

Jimmie never went outdoors to play with Annie. He was content to remain in the women's ward, teasing the old women by making faces at them and mimicking them. It was becoming more difficult for him to walk, and the tapping of his small crutch on the wooden floor was heard less and less often. May had come, and the air outdoors was fragrant with lilacs, when one morning, as Annie was helping him to dress, he fell back on his bed, screaming with pain.

The old woman in the next bed said crossly, "Didn't you hear him crying in the night? He kept me awake."

Later that morning the doctor came, and Annie sat fearfully watching as he ran his hands over her brother's thin little body. The lump on Jimmie's hip had grown much larger. Whenever the doctor touched it, the little boy moaned, "It hurts! It hurts!"

Finally the doctor straightened up and turned to Annie. "Little girl," he said gently, "your brother will soon be going on a journey."

Annie was not sure what he meant. But whatever he

meant, she and Jimmie would be separated. She flew at the doctor, kicking and screaming. An attendant came running and threatened to send her out of the ward. That quieted her instantly.

Jimmie did not get up again, and Annie spent the next few days sitting beside his bed, afraid that, if she left him, they would take him away. At night, after Jimmie was asleep, she would drop off herself into the deep sleep of exhaustion. It did not last through the night, however, for once or twice she would wake up with a start and reach out to touch Jimmie's bed. One night she reached out—and Jimmie's bed was gone.

Annie started to get out of bed, but for a second she was trembling so violently that she could not. When a bed was wheeled out of the ward, it was taken to one place only. Her heart pounding wildly, she stumbled to the door under the flickering light and opened it. Groping in the dark, she found the foot of the narrow iron bed and held onto it for support. Her legs were trembling so that she could hardly stand. She shook herself and felt her way along the side of the bed. There was a sheet, covering something. She lifted it and placed her hand on Jimmie's cold little body.

Her screams wakened everybody. An attendant rushed in and tried to pull her away, but Annie held Jimmie in her arms and would not let go. Another attendant came, and the two of them dragged her out into the ward and tried to put her to bed. But Annie fought them so hard, kicking, scratching, biting, that they finally dropped her on the floor and left her there. Annie became quiet, trying to hold her breath, hoping that if she held it long enough, she would die.

One of the old women crawled painfully out of her bed, hobbled over and tried to lift Annie up off the floor. The effort made her groan with pain. The groan roused the child, and she got up and helped the woman back to her bed. She had Annie sit beside her on the bed, stroked her tousled hair and tried to comfort her. The tears came, and for a long time Annie sat there, weeping quietly, while the old woman whispered to her about God and Heaven.

As soon as it was light, Annie went back to the dead house, but the attendant would not let her in. "Go and get dressed," she directed. Annie dressed quickly and returned. But again the attendant turned her away, telling her to go and wash her hands and face.

"After breakfast," she said, "we'll let you see your brother if you'll be good and not make any trouble."

When they finally did let her in, they made her sit down in a chair before they turned back the sheet. The light in the dead house was dim; it had only one small window. But even Annie's clouded eyes did not need much light to see Jimmie's dark curls and his white face, thin and bony and weazened, like the face of a little old man. Suddenly she jumped up, put her arms around him and covered his face with kisses.

The attendant put a firm hand on her shoulder. "Come away now," she said. "You can see him again later. You must control yourself. It doesn't do any good to make such a fuss."

The day matron found Annie huddled on her bed, her face buried in her arms.

"How would you like to go out with me and pick some lilacs for Jimmie?" the day matron asked.

Annie jumped up quickly, and together they went out into the bright, morning sunshine. "Pick all you want," the day matron said. Annie picked all she could carry and took them, fragrant and still wet with dew, into the dead house. There were enough to cover Jimmie's body.

She watched quietly when the men came in with the new, unpainted pine box and docilely followed the day matron out of the room when they told her she must leave for a moment. They had placed Jimmie in the box when she returned, but they had left the upper part open, so she could see his face once more, a spray of lilac blossoms caressing his cheek. Then they closed the box, lifted it gently and carried it out. For an instant Annie stood rigid, watching them go. Then she ran after them, stumbling, running into things, for her clouded eyes were blinded even more with tears.

The doctor found her down near the gate. "Would you like to go to the burying ground?" he asked.

Annie looked at him pleadingly and nodded.

They followed the men along a narrow path out to a barren, sandy field, where there was an open grave. They lowered the box into it and started shoveling in the dirt. Annie dropped to the ground and lay with her face pressed against the earth, trying not to hear the scraping of the shovels, the rattle of little stones as they dropped on the pine box.

Their work completed, the men stood talking quietly for a moment, then moved away. But one of them came back, and the doctor came over and spoke to Annie.

"Look, little girl," he said. "Tom has brought you some flowers for your brother's grave."

Annie accepted them in silence—a small handful of shabby, dusty pink geraniums. She looked about, then knelt beside the grave and one by one stuck the stems into the soft earth. Around them, when she arose, were some small, dark splotches in the sand, made by her falling tears.

Quietly she followed the doctor back to the women's ward. Jimmie's bed had been returned to its place. It had been made up with fresh sheets. For a long time she sat staring at it, a lonely, desolate child, trying to make the hardest adjustment she would ever have to make in her whole life.

Ten years would have to pass before Annie Sullivan would find another human being to love as she had loved Jimmie.

CHAPTER III

INTERLUDE

THERE WAS ONE PATIENT in the women's ward at Tewksbury whom everybody respected and liked. She was
Maggie Carroll, so badly crippled that she could not move
her body at all and had to be strapped to a wooden board.
She must have been in almost constant pain, but no one
ever heard her complain.

Annie was drawn to her by her manner of speaking. She
had a soft, well-modulated voice, and she spoke good English, which even to Annie's untutored ear sounded more
pleasant than the coarse, vulgar, often profane speech of
the others.

Some days Annie could see a little better than she could
on others, and then she could dimly make out a pair of
clear gray eyes and finely molded features. The attendants
told each other that Maggie Carroll must have been a
beautiful woman when she was young. But no one in the
women's ward knew anything about her past. She never
discussed it, just as she never complained. God had willed
that she spend her last days on earth in this dreary place,

helpless and in pain, and Maggie Carroll accepted God's will with quiet resignation.

Because they were fond of her, the attendants tried to do more for Maggie Carroll than they did for the others. Maggie could read, and she had a little pile of books on the table by her bed. She could not move her arms and could not lift a book or hold it in her twisted hands. But the handy man made a small rack against which the book could be propped up by one of the attendants. Maggie managed to move one finger enough to turn the pages.

Before Jimmie died, Maggie Carroll would sometimes read aloud to the two children. Even the inattentive, mischievous Jimmie would be quiet, as if hypnotized by her voice. And Annie listened hungrily.

Maggie's books were all about religion, mostly the lives of the saints. The awful persecution, the physical torture inflicted on the saints appealed to Annie's sense of the dramatic. Annie herself was already becoming an accomplished storyteller. But she could not understand why the saints accepted all their suffering so willingly, even joyously, and never tried to break away.

"Anyhow," she told herself, "Maggie Carroll is a saint herself, the best saint of all."

Not long after Jimmie's death, the old woman in the bed next to Maggie Carroll was finally wheeled into the dead house. "How would you like to move in next to Maggie Carroll?" the head matron asked Annie, and a lonely little girl became the new occupant of the empty bed.

Annie no longer played as she had when Jimmie was there. She never went into the dead house again after the morning he died. She would spend hours curled up on her bed while Maggie read aloud the lives of the saints—

the same stories over and over until Annie knew them by heart.

She had one way of repaying Maggie. Every morning a tray was passed around the ward from bed to bed. On the tray was an assortment of pills—sedatives and pain-killers. Some of them contained a little opium, and these were eagerly sought after by the patients. Sometimes the attendants would let Annie pass the tray. If they gave her any directions as to which patient was to get which pill, Annie paid no attention. She would offer the tray first to Maggie Carroll to take whatever she wanted. She would next take it to the bedside of a blind woman and give her what she asked for. The rest of the patients got what was left.

Sometimes Annie and Maggie Carroll would have long talks, but Annie got less satisfaction out of the talks than she got out of the reading. She could not accept Maggie's philosophy at all.

"We were all born in sin," Maggie would tell her. "You and I—everybody. That is why God has put us here. It is His will, and we must not fight against it."

Maggie seemed to think that God had placed little An-nie Sullivan in Tewksbury for the rest of her life, with no hope of escape. But Annie did not feel like a sinner. And she had a dream—a great big, wonderful dream—although she had no idea how she could ever make it come true.

Sometime before Jimmie's death, one of the old women told her she had heard that there were places where blind children could be sent to school.

"I'm going to one of those schools," Annie promptly announced.

The old woman grunted disapprovingly and told Annie not to get "uppity." No one else paid any attention. One lone, castoff child, a pauper, ward of the state which did not care what became of her so long as she was out of sight! Her chances of getting out of Tewksbury and going to school were too remote to be worthy of any consideration at all.

But from that day on, Annie lived with her dream. She did not talk about it, because the others only scolded her and told her not to be a little fool. But the dream was always there. Some day, somehow, she would get away from Tewksbury. She would go to school and grow up to be a fine lady, wearing beautiful dresses like those worn by the paper dolls she and Jimmie cut out of *Godey's Ladies' Book*.

A few months after Jimmie's death, something happened that made it look as though Annie's dream might be coming true.

A new priest, Father Barbara, took over the pastoral duties at the institution. Unlike his predecessor, a French Canadian whom the women disliked and nicknamed "Frenchie," Father Barbara came regularly to hear confessions and say Mass and showed genuine interest in his forlorn little flock. The old women found comfort in his kindness and in the warmth of his personality, and they felt less lonely and rejected. Annie followed him about like a shadow.

One day as he was leaving he stopped to talk to Annie, gently stroking her unkempt head.

"This is no place for you, little lady," he said. "I'm going to take you away from here."

Annie's spirits leaped skyward. "Can I go to school?" she asked eagerly.

"Perhaps, after a while," Father Barbara replied. "But first we must see if something can be done about your eyes."

Annie pulled herself away from him and began to cry. Twice in the last few months a doctor at Tewksbury had tried to do something about her eyes. She had been placed on a table, with her hands and feet strapped down so she could not fight or kick. An attendant had held her head while the doctor scraped some of the small granules off the linings of her eyelids. The pain had been excruciating, and the eyes were no better. Lately, as a matter of fact, they had grown worse, with bright specks and streaks dancing around in blinding confusion. Struggling to see through them or around them, Annie kept blinking and rubbing her eyes, which made them more inflamed. The linings of her eyelids were like coarse sandpaper.

"But I'm going to take you to another doctor," Father Barbara said. "He's a very good doctor, and he knows all about eyes. I think he'll be able to help you. You'd like to be able to see, wouldn't you?"

Annie nodded and wiped away her tears on her sleeve.

"Then you must be a brave girl and let the doctor help you," Father Barbara said. "I hope he'll be able to make you see, so that you can go to school as other children do and learn to read and write."

A few days later Father Barbara came for her and took her to a hospital operated by the Sisters of Charity in nearby Lowell. It was February, just about a year since Annie and Jimmie had arrived at Tewksbury.

Father Barbara was chaplain of the hospital, and he came to the ward to see Annie early in the morning before they took her to the operating room.

"You're not afraid any more, are you, Annie?" he asked.

Annie managed to shake her head in apparent agreement. But she did not mean it.

In the gleaming, spotless operating room, the doctor in

white went to work on her eyes. But before he started he put drops in them.

"Cocaine," he said, "so it won't hurt."

Again her hands and feet were strapped down.

"If you started to thrash around and fight me, my hand might slip," the doctor said. "We can't let that happen. Now let the Sister hold your head perfectly still. This isn't going to hurt much."

The ordeal turned out to be less painful for Annie than the first two, back at Tewksbury, had been. The cocaine made her eyes feel numb, and she realized that the doctor was trying not to hurt her. Sometimes she would squirm a little, and the doctor would let her rest.

"Now," he would say softly, "just a little more here."

After what seemed like a year to Annie, he finished, and a very tired child was taken back to the ward with her eyes bandaged.

The operation might have been more successful had it not been for something that happened in the ward the next day. A woman, so badly burned that she died after a few hours, was brought in and placed in the bed next to Annie.

Annie could see nothing, of course, but she could smell the burned cloth and scorched flesh. The woman's screams and the uproar in the ward frightened her as she had never been frightened in her life before. She became hysterical and had managed to rip the bandages off her eyes before she was taken away, into another ward. At any rate, when the final bandages were removed, the specks and streaks were gone, but her vision was badly blurred, worse than it had ever been before.

Annie remained in the hospital all through the spring and early summer, while the doctor treated her eyes. It was the most pleasant time she had ever known. The

Sisters were kind to her, gentle and cheerful. They let her help them in little tasks around the wards, and they sometimes took her with them when they carried baskets to the poor.

Also, she spent a great deal of time with Father Barbara. Sometimes they would sit in a pew in the chapel, next to the hospital, and pretend they were listening to a sermon. Sometimes they would go around to the Stations of the Cross, Father Barbara describing each picture to her and chanting the story that went with it. Sometimes they would take long walks together along the nearby Merrimac River. And sometimes in the evening he would read to her the lives of the saints, as Maggie Carroll had.

Finally the day came when the doctor had finished his work. He could do no more for Annie. It was time for her to leave. Father Barbara, however, had not given up.

"There are some doctors in Boston who may be able to help you," he told Annie. "I'm taking you there. I have some friends in Boston, and you'll stay with them until the doctors are ready for you."

The prospects of more doctors and more operations filled Annie with misgivings. But at any rate she would not have to go back to Tewskbury. And always there was the hope that the next operation might be successful, that the frustrating curtain in front of her eyes would be rolled away.

She stayed only a few days with Father Barbara's friends, then was admitted to the Boston City Infirmary. The doctors there were optimistic, as the doctor in Lowell had been. They started to work on Annie's eyes on a hot day in July.

There were two operations this time, only a few days apart—two more ordeals for Annie. The first one was to remove more of the granules from her eyelids. The second one, longer and more nerve-racking, was to cut away some of the scar tissue from her eyeballs. Somehow Annie managed to get through them. She had no choice in the matter. Again she was taken back to the ward with bandaged eyes. And again she waited, and waited, building up a dream of the day when the bandages would come off and she could see.

But when that day came, and the bandages were taken off, her vision was no better than it had been before. The curtain was still there. Everything looked blurred. And now there were little ridges and scars on her eyeballs.

There followed more weeks in the hospital while the doctors treated her eyes. One day Father Barbara came to say good-by. He had been called away to another part of the country.

It was autumn when the doctors finally told Annie that they had done all they could for her. It was time for her to leave the hospital.

Annie knew what this meant. She would have to go back to Tewksbury. She cried and clung desperately to one of the doctors, but he gently pushed her away. It was hopeless. He could do no more for her.

The autumn day was gray and gloomy when Annie Sullivan—alone this time—rode again through the streets of Tewksbury in the Black Maria. While she sat on the bench in the big dark hall, the man with the green eyeshade made a fresh notation on her record. It was: "Virtually blind."

But Annie Sullivan still could dream.

CHAPTER IV

RESCUE

ANNIE was not put back into the old women's ward upon her return to Tewksbury, but was placed with a group in another part of the institution.

These were not bedridden old women, patiently waiting to die. They were young—some of them not much older than Annie who in April became eleven years old— and they had by no means lost interest in the outside world, which most of them would never see again.

They were there for the same reason the old women were there. They were human discards, cast off by a society that wanted them kept out of sight. There were mild lunatics among them, epileptics and cripples. Some had cancer, some had venereal disease, some were slowly dying of tuberculosis.

Across the hall was another ward, where the unwed mothers came to have their babies. After the babies were born and had lived out the few hours, days or weeks they were destined to spend on this earth, the unwed mothers were sent to a workhouse, from which they would be released when jobs were found for them as maids or scrub-women.

Annie found life in these surroundings much more interesting than it had been in the old women's ward. Daytimes she played with the unwanted babies, who were too weak to give anyone much trouble. Whenever they did become bothersome, the attendants would silence their feeble cries with a few drops of laudanum or paregoric, thereby probably shortening their miserable little lives. When it was cold, the babies shivered under thin, shabby cotton quilts. In summertime they were covered with flies and bitten by mosquitoes. Tewksbury had no window screens.

In the evening, the unwed mothers would come across the hall and join Annie's group around a smoking kerosene lamp set on a post in the center of the room. Here they would regale one another with their life stories—accounts so exaggerated that only Annie and the lunatics believed them.

Out of all the talk, Annie got the impression that men were somehow responsible for the unwanted babies, although she did not know how. There was always a "he" involved. "He said we'd get married." Or, "The mistress was out, and he came home." Or, "He just went away—I don't know where."

Annie was curious, but whenever she asked questions, the women laughed and answered her with ribald remarks which she did not understand. Coarse and vile as they were in thought and speech, they were strangely prudish about explaining the mystery of creation to a child. Annie decided that men were creatures to be avoided, and that having a baby was always a disgrace—the worst thing that could happen to a woman.

Among her new companions, Annie had her favorites.

One was a good-natured Irish girl who waited on table in the superintendent's dining room. She wore a blue dress and white apron, which Annie thought were very elegant. Sometimes she would bring Annie a treat—biscuits, cake and chicken salad, all crammed together in her apron pocket. Annie would eat the soggy mess greedily, licking her fingers. Compared with the lumpy oatmeal, watery stews, rotten fish and rancid corned beef to which she was accustomed, it was pure ambrosia.

In charge of the dark, dreary inmates' dining room was a huge, evil brute whom the women despised and nick-named "Beefy." Whenever they complained about the food—which was not often, because they were afraid of him—Beefy would roar at them, calling them unprintable names and threatening to throw them out.

One day Sadie, one of the pregnant women, yelled back at him, "I dare you to throw me out, you dirty beast!" Infuriated, Beefy lunged across the table at her, slipped and fell. Sadie threw her plate at him, but he regained his feet, seized her by the hair and beat her savagely about her head, chest and stomach.

Bedlam broke loose, in shouts and flying plates, forks and spoons. Annie managed to dump a bucket of hot tea on Beefy as he leaned across the table. Suddenly there was a piercing scream from Sadie.

A couple of days later, they placed Sadie and her pre-mature baby in a pine box, which they carried out to the barren, sandy field where Jimmie was buried.

There might have been an investigation of the incident, but there apparently was none. The superintendent was toiling over a report to the state legislature, in which he humbly noted that, as the result of "careful economy in management and expenditure," the average cost per in-mate per week was down to $1.75. It had been $1.88 when

Annie first came there. Beefy remained in charge of the inmates' dining room.

In the midst of all the degradation and violence in Annie's surroundings, there was one gentle influence. Maggie Hogan, with a terribly twisted back, had been sent to Tewksbury when she was a small child, a cripple and an orphan. Middle-aged now, she was in charge of Annie's group and the unwed mothers. Patiently and quietly, she mothered them all. When one of the unwanted babies died, and there was no priest available, Maggie Hogan baptized it herself, using candles and going through the ritual, which she knew by heart.

Maggie Hogan accepted her dreary fate with resignation, but, unlike Maggie Carroll, she did not attribute it to God's will. It was just one of the hard facts of life, and there was no use in fighting against it. In spirit, you could rise above it to a degree.

"You can't help being poor," she would say to Annie, "but you can keep poverty from eating the heart out of you."

Maggie Hogan was unable to give Annie any encouragement in her ambition to get out of Tewksbury and go to school. So far as she could see, Annie would spend her life there, as she herself had. But she did one thing which, instead of satisfying Annie's desire for an education, only made her want to go to school more than she had before.

In the superintendent's office there was a small shelf of books. Maggie introduced Annie to them and found someone to read them to her. This required some searching, for most of the inmates were illiterate. But there was one girl, Tilly Delaney, who could read, though poorly. Tilly was one of the mild lunatics. She was apparently an epileptic also, for every now and then she would fall down in a fit and foam at the mouth.

Tilly demanded a price for her services. In her dis-
ordered mind there was one spark of hope—a determination to escape from Tewksbury. At nights she would prowl
around the grounds like a caged animal, furtively probing
for a break in the high walls.

Annie made a bargain with her. If Tilly would read to
her, Annie would help her to escape, and the two of
them made the rounds night after night. Occasionally
Tilly would become restless and dissatisfied and would
accuse Annie of not really trying to help her. So Annie
would persuade the night watchman to leave the big gate
open a crack. Tilly would slip out, but before she had
gone many steps, the night watchman would catch her
and bring her back. She had almost made it, she thought,
and she felt better. Next time, she would assure Annie,
she would really get away.

Most of the books were sentimental trash, probably left
behind by some inmate who had been carried out in a
pine box to the desolate burial ground. There was, for
instance, a gem called *Tempest and Sunshine,* about a
violent and wicked brunette and a saccharine little blonde
angel. The rest of the books were lives of the saints, which
Maggie Carroll had read to Annie.

Tilly read in a bored monotone, stumbling over words
of more than two syllables, skipping words, sentences,
sometimes whole pages. Sometimes the reading would be
interrupted by one of her seizures. These frightened Annie at first, but presently she got used to them and would
sit patiently by until Tilly came out of her fit and could
go on reading.

Whatever Tilly left out, Annie filled in from her own
imagination, and evenings she would entertain the group
around the kerosene lamp with renditions of *Tempest
and Sunshine, Ten Nights in a Barroom* or *Stepping*

Heavenward that their authors would never have recognized. Her fellow inmates listened with relish, no doubt welcoming the change from their own familiar stories.

Sometimes Annie would get hold of a copy of *The Police Gazette* or one of the more sensational Boston newspapers. Crime, politics, scandals, she devoured them all via Tilly's halting recital. For anything printed on paper, Annie Sullivan had a hunger as avid as that of a starving man for food. And the more Tilly read to her, the more determined she became somehow to learn to read herself, as the blind were taught to read.

The weeks, the months, the years slipped by in shadowy procession. Annie was eleven years old when she was returned to Tewksbury. She did not know when her birthday was, but at intervals she was told that she was now twelve, thirteen, fourteen.

Her eyes had grown worse. She could no longer distinguish one face from another and could recognize her fellow inmates only by the size and shapes of their bodies and by their voices.

Although her brief sojourn outside Tewksbury had given her an idea of what it would be like to live in clean and orderly surroundings, Annie was not bothered by the filth, the rats, the mice and the cockroaches. She had lived with dirt and vermin most of her life. The vulgarity and the coarseness of her fellow inmates did not worry her. Most people in the world were like that, she thought. She had no sense of shame or degradation. Nobody paid much attention to her, and, since she was undisciplined, she seldom had tantrums.

When she talked about her ambition to leave Tewksbury and go to school, the women laughed at her and told her she was putting on airs. They called her "the Empress of Penzance." Theater going was hardly one of the privileges of women in their circumstances, but the Gilbert and Sullivan operettas were popular and much talked about. Apparently someone in the group had heard of *The Pirates of Penzance.* "The Emperor of Penzance" was a nickname they had given to one of the harmless lunatics, a boy whose job was to sweep the sidewalks. In his topsy-turvy dream world, he was a general leading his armies in defense of his realm. Annie rather liked the idea of being an empress, although she was not quite sure what it meant, but "the Emperor" had no place in her hopes for the future.

Annie Sullivan was fourteen years old and had been at Tewksbury for more than four years, except for the few months she had spent in hospitals, when the Massachusetts State Board of Charities decided to investigate the place. Some of the stories going around the state sounded incredible, but the board appointed a commission to look into them. F. B. Sanborn, a friend of Ralph Waldo Emerson, was its chairman.

Word of the impending visit was quickly picked up on the inmates' grapevine. They did not expect much of it. From time to time in the past, fashionably dressed lady do-gooders had come prying about. Nothing ever came of those visits.

"There's a man named Sanborn who's head of it," the women told her. "Maybe if you can get to him, he'll pat you on the head and call you a poor little girl."

Annie expected more from Mr. Sanborn. For days she went about in a dream, going over and over in her mind what she would say to him if she had a chance. Annie had never heard of King Arthur and his knights. If she had, she might have pictured herself as a princess imprisoned in a tower, with Mr. Sanborn a knight galloping to her rescue.

Black despair filled her heart at times. How could she, one lone child, virtually blind, apparently destined to spend the rest of her life at Tewksbury, expect Mr. Sanborn to do anything for her? In all the years she had been there, only one outsider, Father Barbara, had shown any interest in her. But Father Barbara had. And so Annie hoped.

On a morning in late September, word went around the wards that Mr. Sanborn had come. He was with a group of well-dressed gentlemen. From ward to ward they proceeded, looking around, asking questions.

They were followed by the worried superintendent, whose answer was always the same: "I know something should be done about it, but I can't get the money."

All day Annie followed them about, staying as close as she dared. She did not know which of the men was Mr. Sanborn. They were all just shadowy figures to her. And voices.

The day wore on. Finally it was late afternoon, and they were down by the gate, about to leave. Annie saw her one chance, her big dream about to slip away.

Suddenly she sprang into the middle of the startled group of men. "Mr. Sanborn!" she shouted desperately. "Mr. Sanborn! I want to go to school!"

"What is the matter with you?" a surprised voice asked.

"I can't see very well," Annie said timidly, frightened now that she was the center of attention. She expected someone to grab her by the arm and pull her away.

"How long have you been here?" the voice asked.

Tongue-tied in her embarrassment, Annie could not answer, and the men moved a few steps away, stopped and talked in low voices with the superintendent.

Annie cried herself to sleep that night, convinced that she had failed. Her last hope was gone.

A couple of days later, however, Maggie Hogan came looking for her.

"Annie! Annie!" she cried. "You've got your wish. You're going away to school!"

Annie had to have some clothes. Somehow a little money was found to buy some cheap cotton cloth for two dresses, one red and one blue. One of the inmates, who did mending for the institution, made the dresses and a couple of coarse cotton chemises. Annie's new shoes were heavy, ugly and too tight, but she would have walked on burning coals to get away to school. Her dream was coming true. Nothing else mattered.   U. S. 1174276

Finally the morning of her departure arrived. The Black Maria was engaged to take her to the railroad station, where her escort, a man from the State Board of Charities, would meet her for the short train ride to Boston, where the school was located.

Annie wore her new red dress. Maggie Hogan wrapped the rest of her wardrobe—the other dress, the other chemise and a couple of pairs of heavy black cotton stockings—in a newspaper and carried the bundle down to the Black Maria for her.

Nobody kissed Annie good-by, although several of her fellow inmates went down to the gate to see her off. As she climbed up beside Tim, the driver, one of the unwed mothers shrilly advised her:

"Don't let any man fool you into thinking he's going to marry you. He won't mean what he says."

But the advice she would remember all the rest of her life was given her by Tim as they clattered along to the station.

"Don't you ever come back here," Tim said. "Forget this place, and you'll be all right."

CHAPTER V

NEW WORLD

IN THE LATE AFTERNOON, Annie arrived at her school, the Perkins Institution for the Blind, in South Boston.

The trip from Tewksbury had not been a happy one, in spite of Annie's eager anticipation.

On the train a stylishly dressed woman noticed her and asked, "Where are you going, little girl?"

"I'm going to school," Annie replied, feeling very important.

"Where are you from?"

Annie did not answer. Although she could not see well enough to take in the details of the stranger's costume, she realized that this woman belonged in her dream world, the wonderful world of *Godey's Ladies' Book*. Tewksbury did not belong in that world, and Annie no longer belonged in Tewksbury.

She could feel her cheeks burning with embarrassment as her escort proceeded to tell the stranger all about her, and she was not made any happier when the woman called her a "poor child" and gave her an apple. Her new dress, which had seemed perfectly satisfactory that morning—it was, in fact, the first new dress she had ever had—was all wrong, she felt. And she tried to hide her feet, in the ugly, ill-fitting new shoes, under the seat. Something happened to Annie at that moment that had never happened before. It hurt to be called a "poor child" by this elegant stranger. She was ashamed of her poverty.

Upon her arrival at the school, Annie was taken to a class already in session. It was a singing class, but the teacher had a harsh, unpleasant voice.

"What is your name?" the teacher asked.

"Annie Sullivan."

"Spell it."

"I can't spell."

A titter rippled around the class.

"How old are you?"

"Fourteen."

"Fourteen years old and can't spell?"

The whole class laughed.

It was not an auspicious entry into Annie's dream world, in which her first few months were to prove difficult and disappointing.

The Perkins Institution for the Blind, when Annie Sullivan entered it, was the most famous school for the blind in this country. It was founded by Dr. Samuel Gridley Howe, husband of Julia Ward Howe, who wrote *The Battle Hymn of the Republic*.

Dr. Howe had been dead several years when Annie arrived, and his place as head of the school had been taken by his son-in-law, a young Greek named Michael Anagnos.

Julia Ward Howe, for whom the American public had a kind of reverence, maintained her husband's interest in the school and spent a good deal of time there, giving it prestige that extended far beyond Boston and New England.

Since all the children and some of the teachers were blind, courses were taught in raised print and in Braille, the "dot language" of the blind. In addition to reading, writing, English literature, arithmetic, geography and history, all the girls learned to knit, crochet and do fine needlework. Most of the students attended the school for six years.

The children came mostly from New England, sons and daughters of farmers, well-to-do businessmen, doctors, lawyers, clergymen. Only a few were charity pupils, as Annie was. Their sheltered backgrounds could hardly have been more unlike Annie's if she had landed in their midst from the planet Mars. Although she had come through the years at Tewksbury amazingly innocent, Annie knew more about the harsh realities of life than her schoolmates would ever learn in all their lives. Even the girls of her own age seemed as infantile to her as the unwanted babies at Tewksbury. And to them, her rough manners, her speech—often coarse, sometimes shocking— and her outlook on life were entirely alien. There was no common meeting ground.

One of Annie's major difficulties, although she did not know it at first, arose from the fact that her name was Sullivan, an Irish name. At the time when her parents had arrived in this country, there had been a famine in Ireland. Thousands of young Irish had come pouring into Boston with nothing but the clothes on their backs. Many of them had not even been able to raise the money for their passage and had to work it out after they got here.

Naturally they had to take work where they could get it, as day laborers and servants. Many of them were illiterate. In Ireland during those bad years, it was hard enough to keep body and soul together, let alone trying to get an education. Thrifty New Englanders found them a highly satisfactory source of cheap labor. Since they performed the most menial tasks, they were regarded as social inferiors. Italians, Portuguese, Eastern Europeans and other immigrants coming later would be in the same situation.

Annie arrived at Perkins wholly unaware that there was any stigma attached to being Irish. Practically all the people she had ever known were Irish and proud of it. Poor and illiterate though they might be, they handed down to their children lofty tales of the ancient kings of Ireland. They carried in their hearts a fierce love and longing for their homeland. It took Annie some time to find out that being Irish made her socially unacceptable to the smug little New Englanders by whom she was surrounded.

Another source of her troubles was the fact that she was so far behind in her classes. She had to start way down at the bottom, weaving mats, which she loathed. A great big fourteen-year-old down among the first-graders. They called her "Big Annie," and the nickname stuck for a long time. Impatient as she was to get ahead, Annie's reach exceeded her grasp. She would make ridiculous mistakes in class, and the other children, and sometimes the teachers, would laugh at her.

The other girls practiced on Annie an exquisite kind of torture that girls have undoubtedly inflicted on girls since time began. It is called "having secrets." They would gather in little groups, whispering and giggling. Several times at first Annie confronted them, demanding to know what they were laughing at. Stifling their giggles, they replied with elaborate innocence, "Oh, nothing."

Her resentment and frustration made Annie a problem for her teachers. Since nobody had ever really tried to discipline her before, she rebelled at taking orders from these austere, critical spinsters, so colorless compared to the women she had known at Tewksbury. She was rude, and she was disobedient. Several times during her first year, she would have been expelled from the school had there been any place to send her except back to Tewksbury. Even the most annoyed and discouraged among her teachers could not bear to do that to her.

The result of all her difficulties was that Annie withdrew into herself, a lonely, unhappy misfit. Her dream world was proving to be a cruel disappointment. Night after night she cried herself to sleep in the first nightgown she had ever owned. A teacher had borrowed one for her from one of the other girls the first night she was there. Annie Sullivan was homesick—homesick for Tewksbury.

The children at Perkins were housed in pleasant cottages, with a fine view of Boston harbor, which of course none of them could see. Living in the cottage to which Annie was assigned was a silent middle-aged woman who rarely left her room. She was Laura Bridgman, blind, deaf and dumb.

Many years before Annie was born, more than forty years before she entered the Perkins Institution, Dr. Samuel Gridley Howe and Laura Bridgman, then a child, were famous the world over. Dr. Howe had succeeded in communicating with little Laura, the first time anyone had ever been able to communicate with a person who was blind, deaf and dumb.

Laura was seven when Dr. Howe discovered her, the child of a farmer in New Hampshire. Scarlet fever when she was three had left her imprisoned within an impenetrable wall of darkness and silence. She could communicate with no one. No one could communicate with her.

Dr. Howe took her to the Perkins Institution and set

to work trying to find some way of getting through to her. The method he devised was by use of the manual alphabet, the "finger language" by which the deaf and dumb who are not blind talk to each other. Since Laura was blind, he spelled words with his fingers into the palm of her hand and taught her to spell them back to him.

At first, of course, the words had no meaning for her, and it took many months of careful, patient, tedious effort before the moment arrived when it dawned on Laura that the finger letters K-E-Y in her palm meant the object, a key, which she held in her other hand—that everything she touched had a name.

Laura learned to read and write as the other blind children did, and to do beautiful, intricate needlework, but she never progressed far beyond that point. Unable to cope with the outside world, she was unhappy away from the school, which had become her home. A fund was established to permit her to stay on at the school. She was fifty years old when Annie arrived there—a silent middle-aged woman all but forgotten by the public which had marveled at the "miracle child" forty years ago.

All the children were taught the manual alphabet so that they could communicate with Laura. Most of them were bored, for Laura had no knowledge of conversational, idiomatic English, and the sentences she spelled out with her fingers were stilted, the meaning sometimes obscure. But Annie was fascinated, and Laura Bridgman became the first friend she made after leaving Tewksbury.

For hours they would sit together in Laura's room, in silence, Annie spelling into Laura's palm the day's happenings, the school gossip, things she was reading and stories that had been read to her, including the lives of the saints.

Laura, in her queer, stilted English, would spell out

her thoughts and her troubles into Annie's hand: "I hate to go without my best friend. She kept weeping many times until she left me the ninth of November. She gave me a very beautiful and pure breast pin before I parted with her. I love her half as much as if she was my wife."

As the months went by, Annie concentrated most of her interest and energy on learning to read raised type with her fingers, and she did so easily and quickly. To be able to read was the thing she wanted most. Annie's teachers were discovering that she could master any subject with speed if it interested her, but could be exasperatingly slow if it did not. Arithmetic, for instance, and Braille. She did not have the patience to learn the series of dots that make up the Braille alphabet. She was never good at Braille. She had to learn to sew, as all the girls did, but it took her two years to make an apron, which any of the others would have finished in a few hours.

The carefully selected books in raised letters or Braille in the Perkins library were few in number—only about sixty—but they were good. As it became easier and easier for her to follow the raised print with her fingertips, Annie haunted the library. There she discovered *Silas Marner, The Vicar of Wakefield,* a copy of *Old Curiosity Shop,* which Charles Dickens had had printed in raised type and presented to the school after he visited the place during his American tour many years before Annie was there. There was poetry, too, the poems of Lord Byron, Longfellow's *Evangeline,* Milton's *Paradise Lost.* Even through her searching fingertips Annie got the rhythm, the beauty of the words, and began to acquire a taste for poetry and good English that would stay with her for the rest of her life.

What to do with Annie Sullivan became a problem as the summer vacation approached. The other children all went home for summer vacations, and the school was closed. Even Laura Bridgman returned to New Hampshire to stay with relatives. There seemed to be no place for Annie except Tewksbury, and even Tewksbury did not want her as a summer transient. The teachers were opposed to sending her back there, anyway. Finally one of the teachers found a summer job for her doing light work in a rooming house in Boston. It turned out to be a most fortunate experience for Annie.

One of the roomers, a young man, felt sorry for her at first, then discovered that she had an unusually quick, alert mind. Amused by her gift of storytelling, he talked with her and sometimes read the newspapers to her.

One day he remarked, "I think I know of a place where they might be able to do something about your eyes."

Annie was not impressed. She had heard that sort of talk before. But she agreed to go along when the young man arranged for one of the servants at the rooming house to take her to see young Dr. Bradford, at the Carney Catholic Hospital.

"I'd like to operate on those eyes," Dr. Bradford said after he had examined them.

"But I've had operations before," Annie protested. "They didn't do one bit of good."

"But let's try again," Dr. Bradford urged. "I think I can help you."

In the late summer, toward the end of the vacation, Annie entered the Massachusetts Eye and Ear Infirmary. As the others had done, Dr. Bradford went to work on the linings of her eyelids, cutting away the hard granules that kept scratching her eyeballs.

"You're not going to notice much difference now," he told her after the operation was over, "except that your eyes won't be so sore and inflamed as they have been.

"I want to treat them for a few months, and a year from now I'll go to work on that scar tissue that has built up on your corneas. If I succeed—well, that will be the operation that will make the difference."

A year passed, and Annie returned to the hospital for her second operation. Dr. Bradford was hopeful, and to Annie the passage of the days before the bandages could be removed was agonizingly slow. Finally one morning in the hospital ward, the bandages were cut away.

"Open your eyes, Annie," Dr. Bradford said.

Almost afraid to do so, Annie opened her eyes—and almost jumped out of bed.

"What can you see, Annie?" the doctor asked.

"I can see you!" Annie cried, almost shouting. "I can see you! I can see your eyes and your nose and your mouth and your hair! I can *see!*"

Her glance raced around the ward—to the window, no longer just a white space but definitely a window, through which she could see a patch of blue sky; to the other patients in their beds, back to Dr. Bradford and the smiling nurse in white at his elbow.

The pictures were a little blurred, but beautiful beyond description to a sixteen-year-old girl who had not seen them so clearly since she was a small child. Annie Sullivan had stepped into a new world—a world she had never hoped to enter back in the days at Tewksbury. In her dream world she had expected always to be blind, but able to go to school and learn to read as blind children are taught to read.

"That's enough—rest them a bit," Dr. Bradford cautioned. "They're weak. They'll have to get used to working. You must take good care of them."

By Dr. Bradford's standards, the operation was incomplete. There were still ridges of scar tissue on Annie's eyeballs. He would have to treat them and perhaps operate again sometime in the future.

But to Annie Sullivan when she finally left the hospital —not with the slow, shuffling gait of the blind, but walking swiftly and confidently, with springs in her feet—it was the most wonderful operation in all medical history. Her respect for doctors amounted to veneration.

CHAPTER VI

VALEDICTORIAN

Strictly speaking, Annie should not have been permitted to return to the Perkins Institution for the Blind following the successful operation on her eyes.

Only the hopelessly blind were eligible for admission. While her vision was by no means normal, Annie Sullivan could no longer be classified as "virtually blind."

Again, however, the old question of what to do with her arose. Annie at sixteen was still a minor, still a ward of the state, still a pauper, unequipped to earn her living. But nobody wanted to send her back to Tewksbury.

So at Perkins, Annie remained, a charity pupil, arrayed in hand-me-downs which her teachers begged from philanthropic-minded ladies of Boston. She had been at the school two years and had four more to go.

Gradually a change was coming over Annie. She still had a fiercely independent spirit that would not readily accept discipline from her elders. The fact that a teacher said a thing was so did not make it so. She questioned everything. But she was learning to conform to the ways of her classmates. Her manners and her speech had improved. She was getting along better with both teachers and students.

In addition to her own gradual conformity, other factors contributed to making Annie's lot at the school happier than it had been at first. For one thing, the girls her own age, who had rejected her so mercilessly, had received their diplomas and left. Annie was several years older than the other students in her class, but they had grown used to her. They no longer called her "Big Annie."

Another reason undoubtedly was that, after she regained her sight, Annie was always willing to take her classmates on little excursions into Boston, something the teachers seldom had time to do. To get away for a few hours means as much to a blind child at boarding school as it does to a child who can see.

Annie had a way with the smaller children, especially the new arrivals. The sight of a woebegone, tearful little face brought back to her vividly a time when she, too, was homesick—homesick for Tewksbury. She played with them, and she comforted them. The teachers, observing this, sometimes asked her to assist them in the lower grades.

But a deeper, more important change was taking place in Annie. It could be attributed to the influence of wise, patient Miss Mary Moore, her English teacher.

Annie's friendship with Miss Moore began after an incident that almost sent her back to Tewksbury. It happened in spelling class during her second year. Annie did not have the patience to learn to spell. So long as she could make herself understood on paper, she could not see that it made any difference how the words were spelled!

Perhaps with the idea of shaming her into doing better, the teacher with sarcastic exaggeration would spell back the words as she had misspelled them. This would send the class off into squeals of laughter.

Finally one day Annie's temper exploded. "Laugh, you silly things!" she stormed at her classmates. "That's all you can do, to the queen's taste!"

Annie had not meant to refer to the teacher. "To the queen's taste" was just an expression she had picked up somewhere. But the teacher took it as an insult and ordered her to leave the room and sit on the stairs outside until the class was over.

Furious, Annie jumped up and banged into one of the desks. Whereupon the teacher indignantly directed her to come back and leave the room quietly.

But Annie rushed to the door and, before she slammed it behind her, shrilly announced, "I will *not* sit on the stairs! And I will *not* come back to this class again!"

This precipitated a meeting of all the teachers with Mr. Anagnos, the principal. Mr. Anagnos sternly decreed that Annie would have to return to the class and apologize to the teacher or be expelled. This Annie stubbornly refused to do.

With Tewksbury in mind, some of the teachers intervened, and one of them, Miss Moore, volunteered to take Annie in hand and see if she could tame her. Once a week they had an hour's session together, all by themselves.

Ostensibly Miss Moore was teaching Annie Sullivan to spell and to speak and write correct English. Actually she taught her much more—so much more that all the rest of her life Annie would consider her the best teacher and one of the best friends she ever had.

Miss Moore did not treat Annie as a problem child. In fact, she treated her more as an adult than as a child. Studying her carefully, she realized that, while superficially Annie was as immature as any other youngster in the second grade, she had a knowledge of the seamier side of life that made her adult far beyond her years. Miss Moore, with her sheltered background, could only guess at some of the things Annie had seen and heard at Tewksbury.

When Annie was rude, when she brashly expressed opinions that indicated she did not know what she was talking about, Miss Moore did not correct her. She merely changed the subject, leaving Annie feeling sheepish and wondering if her ill behavior had been noticed. When Miss Moore, without laughing, pointed out her mistakes in spelling and grammar, Annie was fired with ambition to do better. And above all, Annie was brought to the realization that there were a great many things she did not know.

There were times when Annie had an uneasy feeling that Miss Moore was getting her under her thumb, but she was defenseless against her quiet good manners and matter-of-fact assumption that they were friends. Little by little, Miss Moore was disciplining Annie Sullivan's lawless mind.

Miss Moore taught a class in Shakespeare one hour a week. When Annie was far enough advanced to be admitted to that class, it became for her the high point in the week. She would soar out of the class on a magic carpet of romance, great poetry, beautiful words singing in her mind and heart. They read *The Tempest, King Lear, As You Like It, Macbeth,* and Annie Sullivan lived them all.

As a matter of fact, Annie lived everything she read. She loved the history and mythology of ancient Greece. It was her idea that a group of ten-year-olds, struggling with Greek history, take on the names of the heroes. Thus a girl named Eunice became Pericles, a girl named

Lydia became Aristedes and so on. Mr. Anagnos, a Greek, was amused, but observed that Aristedes applied to a girl should be Aristedena. The nickname clung to Lydia long after she was out of school and had become head of the Commission for the Blind in another state.

Annie never could remember just how long it took her to learn to read with her eyes, but it probably did not take very long, for her fingertips knew the shapes of the letters. And now she read everything she could get her hands on, from the classics to the most lurid crime stories in the newspapers. Any book that came her way she read, and the daylight hours were not long enough. One evening Miss Moore found Annie leaning far out of a window into the twilight, her nose literally buried in a trashy novel called *East Lynne*.

Annie Sullivan, blind no more, was entering her fourth year at Perkins when a new matron came to take charge of the cottage where she lived. She was Mrs. Sophia Hopkins, widow of a sea captain. Her home was on Cape Cod, but she had found the place unbearably empty following the death of her only child, a girl about Annie's age.

Wandering aimlessly along the beach one day near her home, Mrs. Hopkins had noticed some blind children, on a holiday from the Perkins Institution, playing in the sand. She applied at the school for a position, to the great good fortune of one untamed, unkempt youngster named Annie Sullivan. It was inevitable that Annie should appeal to her.

No two human beings could have been less alike. Prim, conventional Sophia Hopkins, with her sedate New England background. Willful, impulsive Annie Sullivan, child of Irish immigrants, with Tewksbury as her background. Sophia Hopkins, who needed to mother someone, and Annie, who had never been mothered in her life.

One of the first noticeable changes must have been in Annie's appearance. Mrs. Hopkins could sew, and those hand-me-downs Annie was obliged to wear were a challenge to her. They could at least be made to fit properly, even though the colors and materials might not be very becoming!

A big change took place at the end of Annie's third year at the school. She no longer had to look around for a summer job in a rooming house. Mrs. Hopkins took her home with her, to Cape Cod, as she did every summer thereafter.

There must have been times when Mrs. Hopkins was shocked and dismayed as some of the ideas Annie had picked up at Tewksbury slipped out. And undoubtedly there were times when Annie chafed a little at Mrs. Hopkins's gentle, but determined efforts to make her over into a "nice girl." But Sophia Hopkins needed Annie Sullivan, and Annie Sullivan needed Sophia Hopkins. Out of their need developed a friendship that would last as long as they both lived.

Gradually Annie Sullivan was tamed, and as she advanced into her fourth and fifth years at the school, she steadily became a better student. Nobody was surprised when in her sixth and final year she was chosen to be valedictorian of her class. She had earned the right.

As the important day approached, Mrs. Hopkins took charge. Annie's graduation dress, her shoes, everything she wore that day, Mrs. Hopkins gave to her. It was the first pretty dress Annie Sullivan ever owned. And with it, white shoes, which Annie in her childhood had thought were worn only by angels!

A few days before Annie's graduation, an event took place in the White House, in Washington, that sent feminine hearts fluttering all over the country. President

Grover Cleveland married his beautiful young ward, Miss Frances Folsom. No other president was ever married in the White House.

Day after day photographs of the bride appeared in the newspapers, in Boston as well as everywhere else in the country. It was Mr. Anagnos who first noticed a resemblance between the White House bride and Annie Sullivan. Others could see it, too, and Annie spent hours in front of her mirror, trying to copy Miss Folsom's hair-do.

Mrs. Hopkins decided that Annie's graduation dress should be a copy, not of Miss Folsom's wedding gown, but of the dress she had worn when she was graduated from college. The material was white muslin, with three deep ruffles on the skirt, edged with lace. On the morning of the graduation, she got out her curling iron and fashioned little ringlets, like Miss Folsom's, around Annie's forehead.

Annie was standing in front of the mirror in Mrs. Hopkins's room, staring at herself in ecstasy, when Mrs. Hopkins came in with a beautiful pink sash. It had belonged to her daughter.

"I want you to wear it today," she said and tied it around Annie's waist.

Later, in Tremont Temple, as Annie was about to go up on the platform where she would deliver her address as valedictorian and receive her diploma, Miss Moore appeared with a corsage of pink roses to match the sash and pinned it to her blouse.

Because of the prestige enjoyed by the Perkins Institution, the graduation exercises each year were largely attended. The governor of Massachusetts presided and handed out the diplomas.

There was music, and there were other speeches, but Annie was hardly aware of them. Nothing seemed real to her as she sat on the platform awaiting her turn to speak. The governor had to call her name twice before she managed to get up and advance to the front of the platform. Her mouth was dry, and her feet did not feel as though they belonged to her. But after she had managed, in a trembling voice, to get out "Ladies and Gentlemen," she felt better.

The Boston newspapers the next day, with complimentary remarks, published little excerpts from her speech:

"Self-culture is a benefit, not only to the individual, but also to mankind. Every man who improves himself is aiding the progress of society, and everyone who holds still is holding it back."

There was a nagging worry in the back of Annie's mind that night, however, as she took off her pretty dress, lovingly fingering the lace and the little pearl buttons.

Annie Sullivan was now a graduate of the Perkins Institution for the Blind. She must go out on her own and earn her living. But how? She had come a long, long way from Tewksbury. But she had no training that would fit her for a job. And when she left Perkins, as she must, where would she go?

Miss Moore wanted her to go to a normal school and study to become a teacher. But money would be needed for that. One of the teachers knew someone who might hire her as nursery governess for some young children. But there was nothing definite. Where did people go when they had no home and could not support themselves?

"I *won't* go back there!" she told herself fiercely. "I *won't!* I *won't!*"

Shaking herself angrily, she began to put away her finery. With her face towel she wiped off her white shoes, wrapped them in tissue paper and put them back in their box. She put her corsage in a glass of water and carefully smoothed out the pink sash.

"I wonder if I'll ever have a chance to wear it again," she thought.

Annie was staying with Mrs. Hopkins on Cape Cod when a letter came from Mr. Anagnos, asking her to read an enclosed letter and let him know if she was interested. The enclosure was from a gentleman in Alabama. It was a sad letter about his six-year-old daughter, who was deaf, dumb and blind. Could the Perkins Institution recommend a teacher who could help her?

The little girl's name was Helen Keller.

CHAPTER VII

GROPING

"IVY GREEN," the home of Captain Arthur Keller, Confederate veteran, newspaper editor, gentleman farmer and leading citizen of Tuscumbia, Alabama, was set in spacious grounds, at the end of a long driveway.

The afternoon spring sunshine lay warm upon trees and grass and plowed fields, and the good smell of earth was in the air, as the Keller carriage turned into the driveway.

In the carriage with Mrs. Keller was a young woman wearing a gray woolen costume much too heavy for a mild March day in Alabama. Her eyes were red and swollen, as though she had been weeping. Her expression was anxious, tense. Miss Annie Sullivan had arrived to become Helen Keller's teacher.

Annie had not been weeping. Coal dust and cinders on the long train trip from Boston had left her eyes, still tender from a recent operation, badly inflamed. So impatient was she to meet her little pupil that she could hardly sit still in the carriage.

Captain Keller waited on the lawn with a flowery speech of welcome, but Annie scarcely heard him.

When he paused for breath, she interrupted: "Helen —where is Helen?"

"There on the porch, waiting," Mrs. Keller told her.

Annie's weak eyes made out a small figure in the shadow of a vine, and, almost running, she hurried toward it. As she drew near she slowed down, in order not to startle the child. Now she could see her more clearly.

She was surprised at Helen's forlorn, neglected appearance. Her light-brown hair was unkempt, tangled, her face streaked with dirt and tears, her pinafore soiled. Annie would learn presently that on days when Helen was in a bad mood, as she had been that day, she would not let anyone comb her hair or wash her face.

From the bustle of preparation for Annie's arrival— the guest room aired and cleaned, extra cooking being done in the kitchen, her mother's departure in the carriage without her—Helen had sensed that something unusual was happening. Since she had no way of finding out what it was, she was resentful and badly behaved.

As Annie approached her with outstretched arms, Helen leaped at her with such force that she would have knocked her off the porch if Captain Keller had not caught her.

Snarling like a little wild animal, Helen wrenched herself loose from Annie's arms. These were not her mother's arms, as she had expected, but the arms of a stranger.

Her groping hands found Annie's handbag and jerked it out of her grasp. When Mrs. Keller tried to rescue it, Helen flew into a rage, kicking and scratching.

"She thinks there's candy in it," Mrs. Keller panted.

Annie intervened, handing Helen her precious watch, a graduation present from her teachers at the Perkins Institution. Examining this new toy with her fingers,

Helen calmed down. Curious now, she followed Annie into the house and upstairs to her room.

As Annie started to unpack, Helen's grubby fingers were everywhere, into everything.

"Looking for candy," Annie decided.

She recalled having seen a trunk outside in the hall. She led Helen out to it, placed her small hands on it and tried to indicate by a series of pats that there would be candy in her trunk, which would be along later.

Helen seemed to understand, and Annie felt a glow of satisfaction at her first apparent success with her pupil. Had she realized at that moment what the next month would be like, she would have been tempted to repack her bags and go back to Boston.

With only six years of schooling, no training, no experience and a childhood background that would have horrified the Kellers had they known about it, Annie Sullivan was taking on as difficult and complicated a job as was ever undertaken by any teacher. The date was March 5, 1887. Her twenty-first birthday was a month away.

Her own childhood, however, was really in Annie's favor. Annie had never been deaf, but she knew what it was like to be blind, frustrated and resentful.

When the Kellers, in a recital of Helen's misdeeds, told how in a fit of anger she had nearly killed her baby sister by dumping her out of her cradle, there flashed into Annie's memory an incident out of her own childhood. She, too, in a fit of anger, had dumped her baby sister out of her cradle.

Thus was Annie Sullivan equipped to understand Helen Keller far better than her parents ever could.

She did not mention the incident to the Kellers. Mr. Anagnos had told them nothing about her background, and Annie would have died rather than have them know.

Annie's first task was to win the confidence of a miserable little soul who trusted no one because she knew no one. The people around her existed in her imprisoned mind only as hands—hands that were forever trying to restrain her.

Annie had hoped to win her with gentleness and affection. But almost immediately she realized that this would not work. She had been with the Kellers only a few days when Helen, in a sudden rage, knocked out two of her front teeth! Helen could be as dangerous as a ferocious dog.

At times Helen's tantrums were unpredictable, but in general they followed a pattern. Whenever she could not have her own way, Helen had a tantrum.

This tendency was aggravated by the fact that her parents, rather than fight with her, gave in to her, even to the extent of allowing her to go unwashed and uncombed for days at a time. She was an undisciplined little tyrant, ruling the household by physical force.

After a few encounters with her, Annie was forced to the realization that the only solution must be discipline. Understanding as she did the reason for Helen's violence, she set to work reluctantly, hoping that she would not break the child's spirit.

"If anyone had ever really cared enough about me when I was a child to discipline me," she told herself in justification, "I might have been a happier child."

Their longest and most violent battle occurred one morning at the breakfast table. No one had ever tried to teach Helen to sit at the table and eat from her own plate with a spoon. Instead, she would run around the table, grabbing food off other people's plates and the dishes that were being passed while the family went on eating and talking as though nothing extraordinary was happening.

That morning Helen started to grab some food off Annie's plate. Annie pushed her greasy hands away. Helen tried it again, and Annie slapped her. Whereupon Helen threw herself on the floor, kicking and screaming. Annie lifted her up, set her down hard on a chair, forced a spoon into her hand and started to help her scoop up some food on it.

Helen threw the spoon on the floor. Annie dragged her down off the chair, made her pick up the spoon, set her back on the chair and started over again. But Helen hurled the spoon to the floor and threw herself on top of it.

At this point Captain and Mrs. Keller, who had been watching in horrified silence, got up and left the room, breakfast unfinished. Annie followed them to the door, locked it behind them, returned to the table and went on eating her breakfast, although it nearly choked her.

Helen jumped up and tried to pull Annie's chair out from under her. When that didn't work, she pinched Annie, and Annie slapped her. This was repeated several times.

Finally, after another fit of kicking and screaming, Helen started feeling her way around the table. When she discovered that her parents' places were empty, she came back to Annie. She seemed puzzled and placed her hand on Annie's wrist. Raising her fork to her mouth, Annie indicated that she was eating. Helen hesitated for a moment, then climbed up on her chair and docilely permitted Annie to help her eat her breakfast with a spoon. Apparently hunger had won out.

But the battle was not yet over. As she finished eating, Helen tore off the napkin that had been tied around her neck, threw it on the floor and ran over to the door.

Finding it locked, she blazed with fury, pounding and kicking the door and howling.

Annie went over and, after a struggle that required every ounce of strength she could muster, dragged Helen back to the table, forced her to pick up the napkin and started to show her how to fold it. Helen managed to jerk the napkin away from her, threw it to the floor again and herself on top of it.

This time Annie left her alone. Helen's screams finally subsided into sobs, and she let Annie lift her up and show her how to fold her napkin. It was nearly lunchtime when Annie unlocked the door, and a subdued, quiet Helen wandered out into the garden to play.

Annie went upstairs to her room, threw herself on the bed and cried herself to sleep.

A day or so later, when Helen again started to misbehave at the table, Annie seized her by the arm and dragged her toward the door. Before she had reached the door, however, Captain Keller ordered her back.

"No child of mine," he stormed, "is ever going to be sent away from my table hungry!"

From the beginning, there was difficulty with Helen's parents, especially with her father. She very quickly learned to run to her parents for sympathy whenever Annie corrected her.

"I know we shouldn't do it," Mrs. Keller said. "But we feel so sorry for her."

"If I could have her alone with me for a while, I think I could accomplish more," Annie replied in a discouraged tone. "She's got to learn to obey me before I can help her. I can't do anything with her the way she is."

Mrs. Keller came up with a solution. But she had a hard time convincing her husband. At this point, Captain Keller was going around saying he had a good mind to send that Yankee girl packing. And that Yankee girl would not have cared much if he had!

The Kellers, however, were really in desperate straits. Every day Helen was growing larger, stronger and more dangerous. Unless she could be brought under control, she would have to be sent away. And the only place to send her would be to a home for the feeble-minded—and a strait jacket.

With this in mind, Captain Keller grudgingly gave his consent, and Annie and Helen moved into a cottage a short distance from the Keller house.

In the meantime, as she fought Helen's tantrums, Annie worked tirelessly, doggedly, unceasingly to communicate with her, using the manual alphabet, as Dr. Howe had used it with Laura Bridgman many years earlier. Before coming to Alabama, she had unmercifully abused her eyes, poring over and over the cramped, barely legible notes Dr. Howe and her teachers had made as they worked with Laura.

They had had one advantage she did not have. Laura had been a placid, docile child, who had never given them any trouble.

"But Helen is a much brighter child than Laura was," Annie told herself as she nursed her bruises. "I know she is! I've *got* to get through to her!"

She started using the manual alphabet with Helen the morning after her arrival. In her trunk was a doll for Helen. The blind children at Perkins had bought it with their pennies, and Laura Bridgman had dressed it.

Annie smiled wistfully as Helen delightedly cradled the doll in her arms. She was remembering another little girl, practically blind, who long ago had lovingly cradled a doll in her arms, thinking it was her Christmas present.

She took Helen's hand and slowly and carefully with

her fingers spelled into her palm: D-O-L-L. She did it several times, then showed Helen how to form the letters with her own small fingers.

Presently, like an imitative monkey, Helen spelled the word back to her: D-O-L-L. Tears sprang to Annie's eyes as she patted her small pupil's shoulder.

In the cottage the finger-spelling—which Helen seemed to regard as an interesting new game—continued, along with other things Annie found for Helen to do with beads and a ball of yarn and a crochet hook. With these pastimes, Helen seemed more contented. She had fewer tantrums. Although the words as yet had no meaning for her, she learned to spell them with amazing ease and rapidity.

But Annie still had Helen's father to contend with. He was impatient and skeptical. He wanted his child at home. And after two weeks Annie had to give in.

It had been agreed that Captain Keller could look in on Helen every morning on his way to his office, provided she did not know he was there. One morning, a day or two before they moved out of the cottage, he brought Helen's dog Belle, a beautiful setter, with him.

Helen raised her head, sniffed and ran eagerly to the dog. She dropped to her knees, took one of Belle's paws in her hands and began moving her claws about while Captain Keller and Annie stared.

"What's she doing with that dog's paw?" Captain Keller demanded.

There was wonder in Annie's voice as she cried, "She's trying to teach her to spell! Look—she's trying to teach her to spell 'doll'!"

But Captain Keller shook his head. "What's the good of it?" he said bitterly. "She doesn't know what it means any more than the dog does!"

❧

CHAPTER VIII

BREAKTHROUGH

THEY APPEARED to be playing in the water on a warm spring day—Annie and Helen in the vine-covered pump house in the Kellers' backyard.

Helen held a cup in one hand. As Annie pumped water into the cup, she kept moving her fingers in the child's other hand.

They were not playing a game, however. Helen looked sullen, and Annie's expression was pleading, almost desperate, as she pressed her fingers into the unresponsive little palm.

The date was April 5, a month and two days since Annie's arrival to become Helen's teacher. Day after day through that month Annie's fingers had moved in Helen's hand, spelling words—words—words.

Helen knew how to spell them back with her own small fingers, but they still had no meaning for her. And she was becoming bored with what at first had been a fascinating new game.

That April morning had been difficult. Annie was trying to teach Helen to distinguish between two words,

63

"cup" and "water." Since she did not know what they meant, Helen kept mixing them up. She could not understand what she was supposed to do, and she had grown tired and cross. Finally her frustration drove her into a rage, and she smashed her favorite doll, the doll the blind children had sent her from Boston.

To give her a change, Annie led her out to the pump, a place where Helen loved to play. But still the lesson went on, Annie's determined fingers pressing insistently in her pupil's palm, spelling one word over and over again: W-A-T-E-R. W-A-T-E-R. W-A-T-E-R. The cool water overflowed the cup and ran down the child's hand and wrist.

Suddenly Helen dropped the cup. Her body stiffened. For an instant she stood transfixed, holding her breath. Like a bright probing sunbeam, a new thought had penetrated the curtain that had held her mind a prisoner within its dark folds.

She stumbled toward Annie, reaching for her hand. With trembling fingers she started to spell. W-A-T— She had not finished when she felt Annie's approving pat on her shoulder. The expression on Helen Keller's face was something Annie Sullivan would never forget.

Groping wildly Helen ran about touching things and back to Annie. The ground, the pump, the trellis, the honeysuckle vine. And as Annie's fingers moved swiftly in her hand, the child quickly spelled them back. She knew these words! They had been spelled in her hand dozens of times! This was it—the Big Secret that had been withheld from her so long! *Everything had a name!*

She stopped for a moment, looking thoughtful, then placed a questioning hand on Annie's arm. Tears ran down Annie's cheeks as her fingers moved in Helen's eager palm—slowly and carefully, for they had not spelled this word before.

In that shining moment, Annie Sullivan took on a new identity. Henceforth for the rest of her life, to Helen and to everyone they knew, she would be "Teacher." Her whole life would be wrapped up in that one word. And Annie was content to have it so.

The progress of Annie and Helen into the house that day was a slow march of triumph—slow because of interruptions as Helen found more objects to be identified.

She bumped into the nurse carrying her little sister, Mildred. B-A-B-Y? Of course! Teacher had been spelling it into her hand for a month. Lovingly she patted her baby sister, toward whom she had previously felt only antagonism.

To Captain and Mrs. Keller was given the supreme joy of watching their daughter's fingers delightedly spelling: M-A-M-A! P-A-P-A!

By bedtime that evening, Helen Keller had learned the meaning of more than thirty words. And a contented, sleepy little girl snuggled against Teacher and kissed her goodnight. She had never kissed Annie before or permitted Annie to kiss her. A big hole in Annie Sullivan's heart was filled. Never again in her life would she feel that aching loneliness she had felt when Jimmie died.

The breakthrough had come at last. Annie's real job would now begin.

The first problem would be to teach Helen to express herself with those dancing fingers in conversational language, as other people did. Annie would have none of the stilted, awkward, copybook English of Laura Bridgman.

"How do babies learn to talk?" she asked herself as she tossed about that night, too excited and too happy to go to sleep. "By hearing the people about them of course. At first they don't understand a word. Then they pick up a word here and a word there. They keep learning more words until at last—well, they just talk, that's all."

The following day she started in, keeping a constant stream of conversation flowing into Helen's hand. She encouraged the Kellers to do the same thing, and they were now learning the manual alphabet in earnest.

To her delight, Helen responded with enthusiasm. Her eagerness to learn was insatiable.

"Don't feel sorry for her any more," Annie urged the child's parents. "She's not a poor little thing. She's brighter than most children. And I'm going to help her to be as normal a child as possible."

Helen was learning nouns with amazing speed. Next she must learn to make sentences. She would "hear" them of course as Teacher spelled them into her hand, but she must learn to use verbs, prepositions, adjectives, adverbs. Thus it happened that Helen Keller learned to read almost as soon as Teacher could communicate with her.

Annie had brought with her from Boston some cards on which words were printed in raised letters—names of objects, verbs "is," "come," "go," "run," and prepositions "in" and "on" and "to." Spelling was no problem. Helen learned to read as she learned the manual alphabet, not letter by letter, but whole words at a time.

They started with a box and a table. Helen knew these words, and it was not difficult for Teacher to make her understand that the bumps on the card meant the same thing as the word spelled into her hand.

Next Teacher placed the box on the table and on the box the card identifying it in raised letters. Next to it she placed the cards "is" and "on" and finally the card bearing the word "table."

She had Helen run her fingers over them. Helen hesitated, puzzled, over "is" and "on," but she recognized with satisfaction the words she knew.

Helen entered into this new game with delight, and they played it every day, Teacher introducing new words. Teacher had her reward a few days later. She found Helen standing in a closet, holding in her hand a card on which was printed "girl." Strung out beside her on the floor were cards bearing "is" and "in" and "closet." "Girl is in closet." Helen Keller had completed her first sentence without help.

Annie had also brought with her some little readers in raised print. She gave these to Helen, and the child would spend hours going through them looking for words she recognized. Almost every day she would run across new words, to her great pride.

Helen's lessons were not confined to learning to read and make sentences. In the lovely spring weather, she and Teacher spent most of the daytime hours outdoors. With a packet of seeds, Teacher took her to a plowed field and let her feel the warm, upturned earth. Then she leveled off a place and guided Helen's hands as they poked the seeds into the ground. When they returned later, and Helen felt the little plants that had poked their way up, she wriggled with pleasure.

There were little animals for her to meet. Puppies, kittens, colts, lambs, a baby pig which she held in her arms while Teacher pressed her hand against its throat so she could feel it squeal. One day Teacher placed an egg in her hands and let her hold it while a baby chick poked its way through the shell.

There was another aspect of Helen's training to which Annie gave considerable thought. Helen was a sturdy, active youngster, not timid as many blind children are.

Teacher encouraged her to run, romp, play tomboy games. She even taught her to climb trees!

"We don't want her to go shuffling along, always afraid of running into things," she explained when Mrs. Keller expressed some misgivings. "She'll take some bumps, but I won't let her hurt herself badly."

Years later, when Helen Keller was a young woman, people marveled at her poise, the grace with which she moved.

Almost as soon as she started "talking" and reading with her fingers, Helen began to write. This was her own idea. One day she found Teacher laboriously writing a long letter to Mrs. Hopkins. Helen kept bothering her, indicating that whatever Teacher was doing she wanted to do, too.

Finally, to keep her occupied, Teacher brought out a writing board, used by the blind, a heavy piece of cardboard with grooved lines. She fitted a piece of paper into the grooved lines, let Helen run her fingers along them. Then she took a pencil and guided her small hand, printing several times, "Cat does drink milk." She used the "square letter" printing taught to the blind, every letter made with straight lines, including "o" and "q." It is apparently easier for a person who cannot see to make straight lines than circles.

By the time Teacher finished her letter, Helen had covered the page. Her printing was far from perfect, letters slanting in all directions, but she had kept them within the grooved lines. And her jubilant fingers informed Teacher that she, too, had written a letter.

Not so very long after that, Helen actually did write her first letter. It did not make much sense; she had simply strung together in sentences a lot of words she knew. But it was written only six weeks after Helen learned at the pump that words had meaning!

Preoccupied as she was with her pupil's amazing progress, Annie Sullivan did not pay as much attention to the people about her as she might have done under different circumstances. It was fortunate that this was so, for the old quick-tempered, rebellious Annie could have become involved in some heated arguments at the Keller dinner table.

With some surprise she did notice that the topic of conversation was always the same—the War Between the States and why the South should have won it! To Captain Arthur Keller, as Annie years later recalled it, "everything Southern was desirable, noble and eternal." Of course, in his opinion, the South had had the best generals, the finest armies, the only just cause. The fact that the North had won, which he never admitted, must have been to him a queer, inexplicable twist of fate.

But Annie, on her part, did not have the strong feeling many Northerners had about the Civil War. At the Perkins Institution, she had at first refused to believe it when they told her there had been a Civil War, and that General Grant, whom she had decided as a child at Tewksbury was "the government" and a bad man, was a great hero. Her inclination to argue with Captain Keller about the war was not so keen as it would have been in some of her Boston friends.

In Boston those days, Southern aristocrats were referred to as "haughty Southrons," and her friends had given her an idea, albeit exaggerated, of what to expect from them. But she was a little startled when a Southern gentleman at the Keller dinner table, ignoring her presence, declared that he would rather die than see his daughters working for a living!

Captain Keller had two sons by a previous marriage, thirteen-year-old Simpson and James, a young man. James' friends were in and out of the house all the time, but they never invited her to their parties and they ignored her completely. Annie probably would not have enjoyed herself much if they had included her. She was badly dressed, her eyes—over which most of the time she wore protecting dark glasses that Mrs. Hopkins had sent her— were scarred and inflamed, and she did not dance.

Whatever temptation she must have had at times to flare up was checked by her love and concern for Helen. In a way she was in the position she had been in at Tewksbury before Jimmie died. Whenever she started to have a tantrum, they would threaten to send Jimmie to the men's ward. Now she would have endured any insult rather than jeopardize her position as her adored Helen's teacher.

And the Kellers, whatever their opinion of Yankees— and they were never reticent about expressing it in front of Annie—obviously did not feel the same way about this particular Yankee. How they felt, Annie wrote Mrs. Hopkins, describing her first Christmas with them:

"When we came downstairs, Mrs. Keller said to me with tears in her eyes, 'Miss Annie, I thank God every day of my life for sending you to us, but I never realized until this morning what a blessing you have been to us.' Captain Keller took my hand, but could not speak. But his silence was more eloquent than words. My heart, too, was full of gratitude and solemn joy."

As the months sped by, so full that Annie hardly noticed their passage, the education of Helen proceeded. There was Braille for her to learn to read and write. Annie detested Braille herself and was never very good at it, but she taught it to Helen. More books for the blind were printed in Braille than in raised letters.

The circus came to town, and Helen had a ride on an elephant, played with the monkeys, was lifted up to stroke the ears of a giraffe and was taken inside the cage of a tame—and well-fed—young lion to "see" it by passing her hands over its great tawny body.

And there were long walks, with Teacher's fingers spelling sights and sounds into Helen's receptive palm. There were rabbits and there were pigeons, which Teacher tamed so that Helen could handle them.

There were books to be spelled to Helen, poetry and the tales of ancient Greece, which Annie Sullivan had loved when she was a schoolgirl at Perkins.

And there were lessons about the contours of the earth and its geography, taught in the sand on the shore of the Tennessee River! Helen first learned about mountains when Teacher built them for her in miniature out of sand, rivers when she dug channels in the sand and lakes when she built little dams of rocks and poured water in behind them! Out of sand, bas relief maps of the five continents were built.

And always from Helen there were questions, questions, questions. Her capacity for learning seemed infinite!

In 1888, a little more than a year after her arrival in Tuscumbia, Annie decided with some misgivings and reluctance to accept the urgent request of Mr. Anagnos and take Helen to Boston.

It was time, she decided, for Helen to "see" the world. And there were Braille books in the library at the Perkins Institution.

CHAPTER IX

WONDER CHILD

Annie's misgivings about taking Helen to Boston were founded on highly exaggerated reports of her progress that had appeared in the press, due to the enthusiasm of Mr. Anagnos.

Less than five weeks after Helen had discovered that words had meaning, Annie read with indignation a report in a Boston newspaper that her pupil was already speaking fluent English.

"How perfectly absurd," Annie sputtered in a letter to Mrs. Hopkins, "to say that Helen is already speaking fluently. One might as well say that a two-year-old child speaks fluently when he says 'apple give' or 'baby walk go.'

"Then it is amusing to read of the elaborate preparation I underwent to fit me for the great task my friends entrusted to me. I am sorry that preparation did not include spelling. It would have saved me such a lot of trouble."

In a subsequent letter she thanked Mrs. Hopkins for the gift of a little red dictionary.

At the urgent request of Mr. Anagnos, she wrote a

progress report on Helen after she had been with her seven months. Her factual, truthful report was published by the Perkins Institution, with some extravagant interpolations and comments by Mr. Anagnos. Naturally the newspapers became even more interested in the "wonder child."

Their stories apparently did not worry Mr. Anagnos, who seemed to have greatly magnified Helen's achievements even to himself, but Annie was deeply disturbed. One account had Helen working out problems in algebra. Annie had not even started teaching her arithmetic yet!

"When people find out that those stories aren't true," Annie fumed to herself, "they won't believe she has made the amazing progress she really has made. They'll call me a liar."

Mrs. Hopkins then became Annie's only confidante.

"I shall write freely to you and tell you everything on one condition," she wrote Mrs. Hopkins. "You must promise never to show my letters to anyone."

From that time on Annie wrote a long weekly letter to Mrs. Hopkins. Fortunately Mrs. Hopkins kept those letters, for they constitute the only record of Annie's experiments, successes and failures during those first—and most important—months with Helen Keller. On that record is based much of the procedure which is used in teaching blind-deaf children today.

Despite the urging of Mr. Anagnos, Annie never kept any day-by-day record of her work with Helen, as Dr. Howe and her teachers had with Laura Bridgman. Her weak eyes made writing difficult; her weekly letter to Mrs. Hopkins was an ordeal. And Annie was much too engrossed with drawing out her young pupil and watching her personality unfold to bother with writing reports on how it was accomplished.

Annie only half understood Mr. Anagnos' point of view at first. It was important to Mr. Anagnos that the Perkins Institution receive its share of the glory of Annie's achievement. She was, after all, a graduate of the school. Prestige for the school, which welcomed gifts and bequests, was highly desirable.

Only when she could withstand the pressure no longer would Annie give in and write a report for Mr. Anagnos. It was hard to refuse him. Annie herself owed a debt of loyalty to the Perkins Institution, which had rescued her from Tewksbury and had given her her chance. And Mr. Anagnos had been a generous friend. It was Mr. Anagnos who advanced, out of his own pocket, the money for her railroad fare to Tuscumbia, and when Annie, out of her first month's salary, twenty-five dollars, started to pay him back, he returned the money, admonishing her to start a bank account first. After all other persuasive methods failed, Mr. Anagnos had a final trick. He would enlist the support of Captain Keller.

On a morning late in May, 1888, Annie and Helen, Mrs. Keller and little Mildred set out for Boston. Helen's eighth birthday was a month away.

En route they stopped in Washington to see Dr. Alexander Graham Bell. Dr. Bell had been indirectly responsible for bringing Annie and Helen together.

Months before they ever heard of Annie Sullivan, the Kellers did hear of a renowned eye specialist in Baltimore, and they hopefully took Helen to him. The eye specialist could do nothing for her, but he knew of a man in Washington who might be able to do something about her deafness.

That man was Dr. Bell, who throughout his career gave lavishly of his time and his money to efforts to help the deaf. As a matter of fact, he was trying to make a hearing aid when he invented the telephone.

Dr. Bell examined Helen's ears and shook his head. He took her on his lap and let her play with his watch while he sadly told her parents there was no hope. But he had heard of the Perkins Institution and of Dr. Howe's success with Laura Bridgman. So at his suggestion, Captain Keller wrote to the school, and Annie Sullivan became Helen Keller's teacher.

Captain Keller's grateful letter after Helen's release started a correspondence through which Dr. Bell had been kept informed of her progress. He had also read Annie's report, with Mr. Anagnos' interpolations and comments, and the newspaper stories.

Annie's meeting with Dr. Bell was the beginning of a friendship that would last the rest of their lives. But it started somewhat awkwardly for Annie. Dr. Bell was charmed with Helen, who had developed into a most appealing, lovable child.

"What method do you use, Miss Sullivan?" he asked, smiling as he watched Helen's small fingers fluttering like birds as they spelled questions.

"M-m-method?" Annie stammered, her face red with embarrassment. "I—well, I don't really have any method. I just keep trying new things as I think of them. Some of them work. Some don't."

Method or no method, Dr. Bell was enthusiastic about what Annie had accomplished. One thing that amazed him was Helen's facility in the use of the article "the" and such abstract words as "love," "happy," "good," "bad" and so on. This was not difficult for Annie to explain.

"She learned to use the word 'the,'" she said, "by having it spelled constantly in her hand. I've always used complete sentences with her since her vocabulary became extensive enough to permit it. No baby talk. She learned to use 'the' from hearing it, as any normal child does.

"Other words she has learned from association. One day when she was crying, I put my arms around her and said, 'Teacher is sorry.' She has used the word ever since.

"One day I asked her a question she couldn't answer easily. While she was pondering, I tapped her on the forehead and spelled T-H-I-N-K. She got the idea and started using that word correctly, too."

So pleased was Dr. Bell that in an article published later, he wrote:

"The great problem that confronts us in this country is how to impart to a deaf child a knowledge of idiomatic English. It must be admitted by all who have come into contact with Helen Keller that this problem has been solved in the case of one deaf child."

Again and again in later years, Dr. Bell gave encouragement and staunch support to a beleaguered and heartsick Annie.

When a famous child visits a famous man, reporters find out about it. All the Washington newspapers carried stories about Helen. Everyone was interested in her, including President Cleveland, who invited Helen and Teacher to the White House to meet him. No record of their conversation was kept, but Helen's comment as they drove away may give an inkling.

"Mr. Cleveland was very glad to see me," her fingers spelled happily.

For Annie the visit was in one way disappointing. Mrs. Cleveland, heroine of her schoolgirl days, was not at home.

Helen's first visit to Boston was too brief for the full impact of her fame to hit Annie as hard as it would later. There was, of course, a great deal of publicity, and Helen was the star at the Perkins school commencement, where she read a poem with her fingers, Annie translating it simultaneously. People gushed over her, wept over her and wrote poems about her.

Helen, however, was unaware of it and thoroughly enjoyed herself playing with the blind children, who knew the manual alphabet, and browsing in the school library, which added more volumes in Braille each year. She was as eager to read as Annie had been when she was a blind child, and she would tackle any book, no matter how little of it she understood.

Annie learned on that visit that keeping Helen from getting spoiled by all the adulation that was heaped upon her was not going to be any problem. Since only those who knew the manual alphabet could communicate with her, and hardly anyone knew the manual alphabet, Helen heard only what Teacher chose to spell into her hand. That did not include any of the extravagant compliments. Fortunately, from Teacher's point of view, Mr. Anagnos did not know the manual alphabet!

After a brief stay in Boston, Annie and Helen spent the summer with Mrs. Hopkins on Cape Cod, where Helen learned to swim and Annie noted wryly that some of Mrs. Hopkins' neighbors, who had never paid any attention to her when she was a charity pupil at the Perkins Institution, now greeted her as an old friend.

Annie's eyes were bad, and she made a trip to Boston to have them treated, leaving Helen with Mrs. Hopkins. Since she was matron of the cottage where Laura Bridgman lived, Mrs. Hopkins knew the manual alphabet, and while Annie was away she got out some books of fairy stories that had belonged to her daughter and read them to Helen.

In the autumn, Annie and Helen returned to Tuscumbia. Helen remained there a year, but by the following spring, Annie's eyes had grown so much worse that she had to go back to Boston for another operation. She was away three and a half months—her longest separation from Helen until many years later, when Helen was in her forties and Annie in her fifties.

Helen's education had progressed to the point where that fall she started having regular lessons with Teacher, in geography, zoology, reading and arithmetic. Mastering arithmetic was a towering achievement for a child who could neither see nor hear. Let anyone who doubts it try to do fractions without a pencil. Often Helen would come up with the answer while Teacher was still struggling with the problem on paper. Annie herself could not account for it, except for the fact that Helen had a most unusually retentive memory. Also, since she could not see or hear, she was not distracted by things happening around her.

Upon her return from Boston, Annie decided to take Helen back there that winter. Helen had reached the stage where she needed a good, solid groundwork in her education. And Annie was always painfully aware of the gaps in her own education.

Later, when Helen realized that Annie had eye trouble, she could not understand why she spent practically all of her leisure time with her nose in a book. Sometimes she would snatch the book out of her hands and drag her off for a walk. She thought Teacher was reading for pleasure. But Teacher was reading to keep ahead of her pupil.

Boston those days was called "the Athens of America." Almost every American author of distinction had lived and written there: Hawthorne, Longfellow, Thoreau, at "Walden," near Boston, Ralph Waldo Emerson. James Russell Lowell, John Greenleaf Whittier and Oliver Wendell Holmes were still writing when Helen was a child in Boston.

In Boston, Annie told herself as she tried to allay her misgivings about the publicity which followed Helen wherever she went, she herself might find inspiration and books that would help with her own education. And Helen would have the advantages of the Braille library at Perkins.

Annie's worry about the attention Helen would attract proved well founded. That winter, and for several winters thereafter, Helen Keller was Boston's most publicized celebrity, and the demands upon her time and her strength would have exhausted her if Annie had not weeded them out. The weeding-out process was not simple. Boston society matrons, on the lookout for celebrities to grace their drawing rooms, deluged the child with invitations. Sometimes they would fail to invite Annie, overlooking the fact that, since they did not know the manual alphabet, they had no way of communicating with Helen.

The word "exploitation" was not so commonly used those days as it is now, but while Annie may never have used the word, she knew its meaning.

"What do they want with my little Helen?" she would ask herself. "Just something to attract attention to themselves. They want to exhibit her, as a freak. Well, they shan't—not if I can help it!"

So Annie would turn down the invitations, which did not make her popular with "the Brahmins," as the rich and socially prominent families in Boston were called.

An incident that winter contributed further to Annie's unpopularity. After a great deal of pressure, she granted an interview to a reporter. Innocently she told him that she was entirely responsible for Helen's education. It was true, and Mr. Anagnos had said so many times publicly.

But the abuse Annie took after that interview left a scar that never quite healed. People called her conceited, an ingrate, unappreciative of all that the Perkins Institution had done for her. Latent jealousy on the part of some of the teachers at the school came out into the open. An utterly miserable Annie Sullivan wrote a pathetic letter of apology to the Perkins trustees. And never again in her life did she grant a newspaper interview.

In the early spring, however, Helen Keller—largely through her own courage and determination—achieved something so startling, so far beyond anything her teacher had ever hoped or dreamed for her, that Annie Sullivan's troubles were pushed into the background, almost forgotten.

CHAPTER X

✖

TRIUMPH AND DESPAIR

"I—AM—NOT—DUMB—NOW!"
The voice was guttural, like the growl of an animal, the words so muffled that there were only two human beings on earth who could have understood them. But those words, uttered so haltingly and with agonizing physical effort, were heard all round the world.

For they were spoken by the most famous child in the world, nine-year-old Helen Keller. It was the second time in recorded history that a child who was deaf, dumb and blind had spoken audibly. And Helen Keller's feat was heralded wherever newspapers were read.

The scene took place in the office of Miss Sarah Fuller, principal of the Horace Mann School for the Deaf, in Boston. It was March, 1890, toward the end of Helen's first winter in Boston. Annie had taken her to Miss Fuller doubtfully and only because of Helen's own insistence.

Long before Helen realized that other people used their eyes for seeing, she became aware that they talked with their mouths and throats. Before Teacher came to her, she would sometimes stand between her parents with her

81

hands on their faces. She would feel their lips move, and she would move her lips, too, but they paid no attention to her. Perhaps she was dimly aware that they were communicating with each other. At any rate, they were playing some sort of game from which she was excluded, and it contributed to her frustration and her resentment.

From the time she felt the vibration of her dog barking and a baby pig squealing in her arms, Helen knew that sounds came from the throat. Placing her hand against Teacher's throat, she learned that Teacher sometimes spoke with her throat and mouth, not with her fingers. She wanted to learn to speak that way, too.

Feeling with her hand the vibrations in her own throat, she knew that she could make sounds. But the sounds she made were so unpleasant that Teacher discouraged her. To pacify her by giving her something else to do, Teacher taught her to read lips with her fingers, no small achievement for a person who cannot see. But reading lips with her fingers was slow and awkward, and Helen was not satisfied.

"Why can't I talk the way you do?" her flying fingers would ask. "Why *can't* I?"

It was a question over which Teacher sadly shook her head. She had no answer.

In the late winter, one of the teachers at the Perkins Institution came back from Europe with a report that a child in Norway, blind, deaf and dumb, had learned to speak audibly. That settled it, so far as Helen was concerned.

"If a little girl in Norway can do it, I can do it, too," Helen's fingers spelled, so rapidly that they almost ran the words together into a blur.

She would give Annie no peace. But Annie had nothing to go on, save a report that a blind-deaf child in Norway had learned to speak. No one knew who had taught her or how. Annie did not even have her address, and it took a long time for letters to travel between Boston and Norway those days. Finally, in desperation, she took Helen to Miss Fuller.

The expressions on their faces must have been in marked contrast the day they walked into Miss Fuller's office—Annie, worried, dreading the heartbreak that awaited Helen if Miss Fuller could do nothing, and Helen, eager, expectant, confident. Miss Fuller was doubtful. She had never tried to teach a blind-deaf child to speak. The difficulties looked insurmountable.

"But we might try," she concluded, noting the expression on the child's face. She had Helen read her lips as she explained to her how to make the different letter sounds.

"We'll try the M sound," she said. "It's made this way, by pressing your lips together as you let the sound come out of your throat. Try it."

After several attempts Helen succeeded fairly well.

"Now let's try the T sound," Miss Fuller said. "You touch your front teeth with your tongue—this way."

At the end of an hour, Helen had managed to make six letter sounds: M, T, P, A, S and I.

"Never before have I seen any child so eager to learn," Miss Fuller said. Still by no means confident that she would succeed, she agreed to give Helen more lessons.

The magnitude of her task can best be illustrated if you try to imagine how you would go about showing a deaf person, who cannot see the movements of your lips, your tongue, the muscles in your face, how to distinguish between the letter sounds. M, B and P, for instance, are all made by pressing the lips together. T and D are both made by touching the front teeth with the tongue. To make R and L, the tongue has to be curled. And there are

sounds that have to be made at the back of the palate, like
K and the hard G. Had Helen been able to see, it would
have been difficult enough. But Helen Keller had only
her prying fingers to guide her.

There were eleven lessons before Helen, straining every
nerve and muscle in her body, uttered that first sentence,
"I am not dumb now!"

"From now on," Miss Fuller said, "what she'll need is
practice. I've done all I can."

That meant a lifetime of work for Annie Sullivan on
top of everything else she did for her pupil. Day after day
during the first months, Helen's determined fingers would
explore her mouth until it was sore, going away back into
her throat until Annie became nauseated. Over and over
and over again, those letter sounds and words—new words
fighting to escape from Helen Keller's throat. Almost
from the first she refused to talk with her fingers any
more, even though Annie had to translate almost everything she said.

In Helen's triumph there was also heartbreak for Annie. Before they permitted her to start making letter
sounds and pronouncing words, Helen should have been
taught how to produce sounds correctly from her throat.
This tragic mistake was not discovered until Helen had
been talking for several years, too late to change the habit
she had formed. As the result, her voice would always be
unnatural, without inflection, the words so indistinct that
it was difficult for a stranger to understand her.

It was not Annie's fault, nor Miss Fuller's, for that matter. Comparatively little was known about teaching the
deaf to speak those days. But Annie never forgave herself.
All through the years, almost up to the day of her death,
she struggled to improve Helen's speech.

Imperfect though her speech was, however, it was a

miracle that she could speak at all, and she became even more famous than she had been before. Ragnhild Kaata, the little girl in Norway who spoke before Helen did, was forgotten. But Helen Keller, the "wonder child," was known the world over.

In Maine, they named a ship after her. In London, Queen Victoria asked a visiting American about her. In Athens, the Queen of Greece wept when Mr. Anagnos read to her a letter he had received from Helen. Annie still had to sort carefully the floods of invitations Helen received in Boston, but there were compensations.

Helen and Annie met Oliver Wendell Holmes when he invited them to have tea with him alone one Sunday afternoon in his study. Edward Everett Hale, who wrote *The Man Without a Country,* said he and Helen were distantly related, and he always addressed her as "Little Cousin." Annie decided it was time Helen received some religious instruction, and she took her to Phillips Brooks, one of the most distinguished clergymen of his day, and sat by translating his words into her hand as he held Helen on his lap. Helen became so fond of him that when she was allowed to name her new baby brother, she called him Phillips Brooks.

Annie and Helen made other friends, not so well known outside of Boston, who gave them a great deal, both materially and in warm, comforting friendship in time of trouble. One was a wealthy industrialist, John Spaulding, whose friends called him "King John." His generosity helped make it possible for Helen to complete her education, and a bequest in his will went into the first home they ever owned.

There were the Chamberlins, with whom Annie Sullivan spent many of the happiest days in her life. Joseph E. Chamberlin was literary critic on the *Boston Tran-*

script. He and his family, including several children, lived near the village of Wrentham, about twenty-five miles from Boston. Their big, rambling house overlooked King Philip's Pond, named after the Indian chief, who was said to have breathed his last beneath a huge oak near the Chamberlins' house. It was while visiting the Chamberlins that Helen had her first toboggan ride, learned to dive and swim under water, paddle a canoe and ride a tandem bicycle with Annie on the front seat to steer it.

Helen's correspondence was heavy. Thank-you notes, in her neat, square-hand script, traveled to many faraway places. People were always sending her things. She was an indefatigable letter writer anyway. A sample is a letter written to the poet, John Greenleaf Whittier, on his birthday, in December, 1890:

Dear Kind Poet:

This is your birthday; that was the first thought which came into my mind when I awoke this morning; and it made me glad to think I could write you a letter and tell you how much your little friends love their sweet poet and his birthday. This evening they are going to entertain their friends with readings from your poems and music. I hope the swift-winged messengers of love will be here to carry some of the sweet melody to you in your little study by the Merrimac.

At first I was very sorry when I found that the sun had hidden his shining face behind dull clouds, but afterwards I thought why he did it, and I was happy. The sun knows that you like to see the world covered with beautiful white snow, and so he kept back all his brightness and let the little crystals form in the sky. When they are ready, they will softly fall and tenderly cover every object. Then the sun will appear in all his radiance and fill the world with light.

If I were with you today, I would give you eighty-three

kisses, one for each year you have lived. Eighty-three years seems very long to me. Does it seem long to you? I wonder how many years there will be in eternity. I am afraid I cannot think of so much time.

I received the letter you wrote me last summer, and I thank you for it. Teacher is well and sends her kind remembrance to you.

The happy Christmas time is almost here! I can hardly wait for the fun to begin! I hope your Christmas Day will be a very happy one, and that the New Year will be full of brightness and joy for you and everyone.

From your little friend,
HELEN KELLER.

The Quaker poet replied:

My Dear Young Friend:

I was very glad to have such a pleasant letter on my birthday. I had two or three hundred others, and thine was one of the most welcome of all. I must tell thee how the day passed at Oak Knoll. Of course the sun did not shine, but we had great open wood fires in the rooms, which were all very sweet with roses and other flowers, which were sent to me from distant friends, and fruits of all kinds from California and other places. Some relatives and dear old friends were with me through the day. I do not wonder thee thinks eighty-three years a long time, but to me it seems but a very little while since I was a boy no older than thee, playing on the old farm at Haverhill. I thank thee for all thy good wishes and wish thee as many. Give my best regards to Miss Sullivan, and with a great deal of love I am

Thy old friend
JOHN G. WHITTIER.

Helen's urge to express herself on paper was not limited to letter writing. She also wrote poems and stories, and before she was ten years old had contributed to *St. Nicholas Magazine,* a children's publication which was popular those days. People were often amazed at the facility with which she expressed herself.

The Kellers were spending Indian summer in the autumn of 1891 at their hunting lodge in the mountains when Helen wrote *The Frost King.* She was inspired by Teacher's description, spelled into her hand, of the beautiful colors Jack Frost had painted with his giant brush.

The Frost King was a fairy story, containing some descriptions of the frozen north and the king's wondrous ice palace of such exquisite imagery that even Teacher was surprised when she read it as Helen had punched it out in Braille. She read it to the family that night at dinner.

"Did you read that in some book?" Captain Keller asked.

"Oh, no," Helen replied earnestly. "I wrote it out of my own head. It's for Mr. Anagnos, for his birthday."

The next day she copied it, in her neat script, took it to the post office and mailed it.

Some months later, the Perkins Institution published the story, along with comments by Mr. Anagnos that made anything he had previously written about Helen seem pale and tepid. He compared the child to Wordsworth, Keats and Aristotle!

Shortly after the story was published, a letter came to the Perkins Institution accusing Helen of plagiarism. Before Helen was born, Margaret T. Canby had written a story called *The Frost Fairies,* published in a children's book entitled *Birdie and His Fairy Friends.*

Miss Canby's story and Helen's story were so alike that there could be no doubt that the child, consciously or unconsciously, had committed plagiarism. Some passages were repeated word for word, and the whole idea of the story was the same.

Mr. Anagnos, very much perturbed, started an investigation. At first nobody could figure out what had happened. Neither Annie, members of the Keller family nor any of the teachers at the Perkins school had ever heard of Miss Canby's book. Finally it was discovered that Mrs. Hopkins had had a copy of the book among some children's books that had belonged to her daughter. She had read the story to Helen the summer when Annie went to Boston to have her eyes treated, leaving Helen with Mrs. Hopkins on Cape Cod.

The question was: Did Helen knowingly steal Miss Canby's story and try to pass it off as her own? Or had it remained dormant in the back of her extraordinarily retentive memory to come out eventually as an expression of her own imagination? And if it was plagiarism, was her teacher guilty, too? Most people thought so.

There followed what amounted to a formal trial for Helen, with four adults, two blind and two sighted, sitting as judges with Mr. Anagnos. Annie was barred from the room. For two endless hours they questioned and cross-questioned the child while in her broken, halting speech she tried to convince them of her innocence. Without Teacher's familiar fingers in her hand, she could not at times understand what they were saying. There was no one who could use the manual alphabet so well as Teacher could.

Finally, the verdict was rendered, and an exhausted, tearful Helen walked out of the room into the arms of her teacher. Two of the judges voted against Helen, two for her. Mr. Anagnos cast his vote for her. Later, however, he recanted and publicly said he thought Helen and her teacher were both guilty.

Some people were kind. Miss Canby said publicly, "I do not see how anyone can be so unkind as to call it plagiarism. It is a wonderful feat of memory." And she wrote Helen a comforting letter, begging her not to worry about it.

To Annie, Dr. Bell wrote:

"We all do what Helen did. Our most original compositions are composed exclusively of expressions derived from others. We do the very same thing. Our forms of expression are copies in our earlier years, from the expressions of others which we have heard in childhood."

And Mark Twain, when he heard about it some years later, said that what they had done to Helen was the worst thing that had been done to a child since the British burned Joan of Arc at the stake.

CHAPTER XI

NEW PLANS

THE INCIDENT of *The Frost King* left scars on Annie Sullivan and Helen Keller that would never quite disappear.

For months, whenever Helen would make an unusually bright remark, Annie, in spite of herself, would think, "I wonder where she picked *that* up."

Helen, when she was a young woman trying to earn her living as a professional writer, would tear a sheet of paper out of her typewriter, saying to herself, "I must have read that sentence somewhere."

Tormented by a sense of guilt—a feeling that she herself should somehow have prevented it—Annie undertook the difficult task of restoring Helen's confidence in herself. They left the Perkins Institution, never to return except for brief, casual visits, and went back to Alabama. All the sparkle had gone out of the child's personality, and she was so pale and listless that word went around that she was seriously ill. Her teacher had pushed her too hard, people said. At that time her teacher was not pushing her at all. Lessons were temporarily abandoned.

Then a request came for Helen to write the story of her life for *The Youth's Companion,* a children's magazine with a very large circulation. And Annie made her do it.

"It's the only way to pull her out of it," Annie told herself over and over. "The child has talent, a great deal of talent. We can't let that thing wreck her whole life."

It must have taken every last ounce of moral courage they possessed for Helen to write that story, under Annie's watchful eye. Finally it was finished and sent off to the magazine. The editors liked it and published it, and there were no repercussions.

They were both at loose ends. To return to Boston was impossible, not only because of *The Frost King* incident, but for financial reasons. Captain Keller had never made much money with his newspaper; he farmed as a gentleman farmer, not commercially, and he had expensive tastes—fine horses, well-bred hunting dogs, a shooting lodge. He had long since ceased to pay Annie's salary, and he never did pay it again. Unless they were financed by some of their wealthy friends, travel for Annie and Helen was impossible.

Annie also felt that the time had come when Helen needed more advanced teaching than she could give her. That Helen spoke and wrote as well as she did was entirely due to the hours Annie spent reading. She read always the classics, the world's great literature—only the best was good enough for Helen. And through her reading she acquired a taste for beautiful English and a mastery of it that she passed on to her pupil. As for Helen, she had already learned to speak and write a little French, having learned it by thumbing through a Braille French-English dictionary she found in the Perkins library!

Several months after they returned to Alabama, Dr. Bell came to their rescue. He gave them a trip to Niagara

Falls, invited them to be his guests at the second inaugura-
tion of Grover Cleveland and in the summer of 1893 took
them out to the World's Fair, in Chicago. The trips did
them good, and Helen became her old buoyant, happy
self, except occasionally while she was writing letters.

Following the Chicago trip, they went to stay with their
friend, William Wade, a magazine publisher, who lived
in Hulton, Pennsylvania. Annie explained to him her
problem about Helen's studies, and he called in one of his
friends, the Rev. John D. Irons, a Presbyterian clergyman, who had studied Latin and Greek extensively. With
him, Helen started Latin, Annie spelling the words into
her hand. Annie had never had any Latin, but she did not
need to know the language. All she had to do was to spell
the words.

"I shall get an education along with Helen," she told
Mr. Wade. "And I can certainly use it!"

The following summer, in 1894, Dr. Bell arranged for
Annie to address a meeting of the American Association
to Promote the Teaching of Speech to the Deaf, at
Chautauqua, N. Y. Undoubtedly he did it to help Annie
win back confidence in herself. But it did not quite work.
At the last moment Annie was overcome by shyness, and
Dr. Bell had to read her speech for her. Some of her hon-
est, forthright remarks will give an indication as to how
she felt about her pupil at that time:

"Much has been said and written about Helen Keller.
Too much, I think, has appeared in type. One can scarcely
take up a newspaper or a magazine without finding more
or less exaggerated accounts of her so-called 'marvelous
accomplishments,' which I believe consist only in her
being able to speak and write the language of her country
with greater ease and fluency than the average seeing and
hearing child of her age.

"It is easier for the credulous to say, 'She is a miracle, and her teacher is another miracle,' and for the unbelievers to declare, 'Such things cannot be; we are being imposed upon,' than it is to make a conscientious study of the principles involved in her education.

"I shall have cause for gratification if I succeed in convincing you that Helen Keller is neither a 'phenomenal child,' 'an intellectual prodigy,' nor an 'extraordinary genius,' but simply a very bright and lovely child, unmarred by self-consciousness or any taint of evil."

She then went on to explain how she had taught Helen and how she believed it was possible to teach any deaf child ease and fluency of expression simply by keeping a constant stream of normal, adult conversation flowing into its mind, subconscious or conscious. She might as well have saved her breath. Helen continued to be the "wonder child," and highly colored accounts of her accomplishments continued to roll off the presses.

At the Chautauqua meeting, Annie met John D. Wright and Dr. Thomas Humason, who were opening a school that fall in New York City to teach oral language to the deaf. They had heard Helen speak and hoped that, with the new methods, her voice might be made more normal.

That autumn, at the age of fourteen, Helen, with Annie always at her side, entered the Wright-Humason school. Then the tragic mistake that Miss Fuller and Annie had made was revealed. Very little could be done about Helen's voice. It was too late. She had acquired a firmly fixed habit of producing sound from her throat incorrectly. Nothing could change it.

Through the generosity of their friend "King John" Spaulding, in Boston, Helen and Annie remained two years at the Wright-Humason school, Helen pursuing studies roughly equivalent to junior high school courses nowadays. Those were the most glamorous years of their lives.

They met everybody—the rich, the powerful, the famous. In the homes of their friends, the wealthy Laurence Huttons, Mary Mapes Dodge and Richard Watson Gilder, editor of the *Century Magazine,* they met such giants in the financial world as John D. Rockefeller and Col. H. H. Rogers, another Standard Oil millionaire, such literary celebrities as William Dean Howells, Charles Dudley Warner, Hamilton Wright Mabie, John LaFarge, Henry VanDyke, Kate Douglas Wiggin and Mark Twain—especially Mark Twain, who would remain one of their closest friends until his death. There were others. Woodrow Wilson, then a professor at Princeton University. And some very famous theater people, Henry Irving and Joseph Jefferson, still remembered by old-timers who may never have seen him, but who heard of his performance as Rip van Winkle. And the first lady of the theater those days, Ellen Terry.

When they met Miss Terry, she kissed Annie and said, "I do not know whether I am glad to see you or not, for I feel so ashamed of myself when I think of how much you have done for the little girl."

It was all colorful, brilliant and breath-taking. But Annie had some bad moments. She was so desperately afraid that something about her wretched background might slip out. In later years she would realize that this was a foolish snobbery. But Annie was still not thirty years old at that time, and the specter of Tewksbury was always with her.

She never talked about it to anyone. Into Helen's palm she spelled charming stories about her beautiful mother, her little sister Mary, her brother Jimmie and her "delightful" father and his stories about the faeries and the little folk in Ireland. Her fears lest the story of her child-hood reach the ears of her new friends in New York proved groundless. Mr. Anagnos and the teachers at Per-kins, even though there was no longer the friendly feeling between them that there had been, kept her secret well.

During her second year at the Wright-Humason school, the question of Helen's future again came up. Helen, at the age of eleven, had announced that some day she was going to Harvard. Obviously she could not go to Harvard. But there is a women's college, Radcliffe, whose students attend classes with the Harvard men and whose diplomas are signed by the president of Harvard.

At the time when Helen made her announcement, An-nie did not take her seriously. She thought she would outgrow it. The idea of a deaf-blind person going through college was too incredible. But Helen did not outgrow it. She was as determined about going to Harvard as she had been about learning to speak orally.

If Helen was going to Radcliffe or any other college, she would have to pass college entrance examinations. Worried and uncertain, Annie talked the problem over with the Huttons, Mark Twain and some of her other New York friends.

Always there was the financial problem. About that time Annie had a battle royal with Captain Keller, who had decided that the way to recoup his lost fortunes was to take Helen out on the road and exhibit her! In his anger because Annie resisted him, he wanted to take Helen away from her. But fortunately Mrs. Keller stepped in, Helen remained with Annie and she was not taken out on the road to be exhibited as a freak! Shortly thereafter, Captain Keller died.

Mrs. Hutton, whom Helen called "Aunt Eleanor," Colonel Rogers, Mark Twain and some of their other friends decided that something must be done to make the future for Helen and her teacher more secure. Their friend, "King John" Spaulding had died. He had left them some money, but their friends thought it should be invested, not spent. Among themselves, with Dr. Bell joining in, they raised enough money to see Helen through college and to provide, they hoped, some security for her and Annie afterward.

The next question for Annie to ponder was how to go about preparing Helen for her college entrance examinations. They would be tough—the same examinations the boys had to pass to get into Harvard. Helen could be tutored, or she could go to a preparatory school. If she went to a school, she would be competing for the first time with children who could see and hear. The children at the Wright-Humason school were not blind, but they were deaf. Against the advice of Mrs. Hutton and some of her other friends, Annie decided it should be a school.

"When she gets to college," she told them, "she will have to compete with students who can see and hear. I think we'd better try it out now and see if she can do it successfully before she goes to college. I think she can do it."

On the advice of Elizabeth Cary Agassiz, president emeritus of Radcliffe, Annie chose the Cambridge School for Young Ladies, which was essentially a preparatory school for girls planning to enter Radcliffe. It was located in Cambridge, near the college.

The head of the school was Arthur Gilman, and from the beginning he and Annie did not exactly see eye to eye. For some reason which she could not explain even to herself, Annie did not quite trust him. From the moment Helen entered the school, it received a great deal of publicity, and Annie knew from experience what publicity could do to people.

Annie had another worry—her eyes. They were never anywhere near normal, and she was having to have them treated more and more often. Helen, at this stage, knew there was something wrong with Teacher's eyes, but she had no idea how bad they were. Annie knew Helen would have a great deal of homework, and it would mean many hours of reading for her weak eyes, since not many of the textbooks she would need were printed in Braille. Helen had now advanced beyond the point at which education for the blind, those days, ceased.

At first all went well. After she had been there a few months, Mr. Gilman wrote an article for the *Century Magazine*, in which he paid Annie this generous tribute:

"I could do little for Miss Keller were it not that Miss Sullivan continues her loving superintendence and follows her with the ministrations she has so willingly rendered all these years."

During her first year at the school, Helen's progress exceeded Annie's fondest hopes. They lived in a cottage nearby with some of the other girls, and that was good for Helen, although she had to spend twice as much time on her homework as they did. Annie went to classes with her and spelled into her hand what the teacher was saying. Mr. Gilman and one of the other teachers learned the manual alphabet. Helen, by this time, had learned to use a typewriter, and she did her written homework on that.

At the end of her first year, it was decided that Helen might as well take some of her college entrance examinations in subjects in which she was prepared. The examinations were held in late June, shortly after Helen's seventeenth birthday.

Annie could not be with her, but Mr. Gilman spelled

the questions into her hand, and Helen wrote the answers on her typewriter. They had to have a room by themselves so that her typing would not distract the other students. Helen passed them all with flying colors and with honors in German and English.

In the autumn of Helen's second year at the school, the difficulties began. The course at the school normally lasted five years, but Helen had done so well that some of her teachers felt that she could finish in three years—two more years. With this Mr. Gilman did not agree, and he insisted on lightening Helen's schedule, over Annie's objections. He said Helen was working too hard, but Annie, who knew her better than anyone else did, knew she was not.

There was some trouble with her work, too. Some badly needed textbooks which had been especially printed for her in Braille arrived late. Helen had started to take Greek, for which she needed a special cylinder for her typewriter. It also arrived late, and she had to learn how to manipulate it. She also had to learn how to construct geometrical figures with wires, on a cushion. But still she and Teacher plodded on.

Finally one day in November Helen had a cold, and Annie kept her in bed. Then trouble really began. Mr. Gilman ordered geometry and astronomy taken out of Helen's program. And without Annie's knowledge, he wrote Mrs. Keller that she was treating Helen cruelly and endangering her health. To Annie, Mrs. Keller wrote:

"I always think of Helen as partly your child, and whilst in this I think first of her, I think of you, and utter ruin to the life you have striven so patiently to develop and round out."

Things went on fairly smoothly for about a month, Annie swallowing her hurt and her indignation. But in early December she found out that Mr. Gilman had started a movement to take Helen away from her.

Annie's first thought was to take Helen, and her younger sister, Mildred, who was also in her care, back to their mother, in Alabama. But Mr. Gilman would not permit it, and he showed Annie a telegram from Mrs. Keller authorizing him to take complete charge of Helen. He also brought up Annie's battle with Captain Keller, who had tried to take Helen away from her.

Mr. Gilman tried to take Helen and Mildred to his home, but, terrified at being separated from Teacher, they refused. They remained in the cottage where they had been living, but Annie was shut out.

Annie Sullivan used to say later that never in her life was she so close to suicide as she was that winter afternoon when she rode on a trolley car across the Charles River into Boston. But she managed to pull herself together, went to spend the night with friends and sent desperate telegrams to Mrs. Keller, Dr. Bell, Mr. Chamberlin in Wrentham, and to Mrs. Hutton.

Upon receipt of her telegram, Mrs. Keller took the next train North. Dr. Bell sent to Boston his secretary, John Hitz, a lovable old man who was deeply fond of Annie and Helen. And Mrs. Hutton wrote Mr. Gilman a letter in which she stated that the money that had been raised for Helen's education was for both Helen and her teacher, and that if it were not spent that way, it would have to be returned!

Mrs. Keller, once on the scene, realized that she had been misled. She took Mildred back to Alabama with her, and Annie and Helen went to stay with the Chamberlins in Wrentham.

Nobody ever tried to take Helen Keller away from Annie Sullivan again.

CHAPTER XII

HAPPY DAYS

ANNIE AND HELEN lived with the Chamberlins for eight months, through the rest of the winter and the following summer. Those were the first completely happy days Annie Sullivan had ever known.

The Chamberlins had a big house, and they were hospitable. Most of the guests were writers and editors, friendly and unpretentious, with none of the stuffiness or snobbishness Annie had encountered in the Boston Brahmins or in the Kellers' friends in Alabama. For the first time in years she was relaxed. Although she still carefully guarded her Tewksbury secret, she must have sensed that it would not matter to these people.

Annie loved good conversation, and the conversation at the Chamberlin dinner table was lively and interesting. She was herself a good conversationalist. Some of the Chamberlins learned the manual alphabet so that they could talk to Helen, and more than once she was told that Teacher was a very fascinating person.

At Red Farm, the Chamberlin home, there were outdoor sports; in the winter, tobogganing. They would load the toboggan on the crest of a steep bank overlooking King Philip's Pond, which would be frozen solid from shore to shore. Someone would give it a shove, and off it would go right through the air, down and through a snow-drift and skimming all the way across the pond on the ice. In the summer, there were gardening, long hikes through the woods, picnics and swimming. Annie learned to swim and dive at Red Farm and to paddle stern in a canoe while Helen paddled bow. Helen learned to dive and to swim under water, with a rope tied around her waist so that she could find her way out.

Annie loved animals. Helen had a series of dogs while she was growing up, and Annie was as fond of them as she was. One of them, a huge mastiff, bit Annie. Captain Keller, over Annie's tearful protest, shot the dog, and Annie was sent to the Pasteur Institute in New York for antirabies treatment. Annie insisted that the dog was not mad, only confused and frightened. It was a new dog, not yet accustomed to its surroundings. She was probably right. At any rate she showed no sign of developing rabies.

There were dogs at Red Farm, and there were horses to be driven and ridden. Annie had learned to ride in Alabama; Captain Keller owned saddle horses as well as carriage horses. Helen had a pony, named Black Beauty after the horse in the book, which children still read and love, and she and Teacher would go off on long rides through the woods. Sometimes, when she was restless and unhappy, as she was after *The Frost King* incident, Annie would take wild rides by herself, recklessly jumping the horse over streams and gullies and fences.

Once during the Wrentham days (Annie and Helen rented a cottage at one of the nearby lakes and spent several summers there after they left Red Farm) someone gave Annie a horse of her own, a beautiful animal which she loved as though it were human. With a book tucked into the pocket of her plum-colored riding habit, Annie would go off by herself, and sometimes she would be found sitting up against a tree, reading for pleasure—which she was not supposed to do—the horse grazing contentedly nearby.

During this period, Annie was able for the first time to indulge her taste for pretty clothes. The income from the fund established by their friends in New York made it possible. Annie, still in her very early thirties, was small and slender. Even her scarred eyes could not completely mar the beauty of her face, the lovely wistful curve of her mouth. She knew how to select good clothes and wear them. Annie Sullivan had at last fulfilled her childhood dream of looking like the women in *Godey's Lady's Book*.

Helen celebrated her seventeenth birthday while they were staying with the Chamberlins. She had grown tall, and she moved with a kind of grace, Teacher lightly touching her elbow now and then to guide her. Her light-brown hair curled in soft waves about her face, and one had to look at her intently before the realization dawned that she was blind. Her blue eyes always stared straight ahead.

Sometimes in letters to her mother or her sister, Helen would describe the new dresses she and Teacher had acquired. For instance:

"We've just had four lovely dresses made by a French dressmaker. I have two, of which one has a black silk skirt, with a black lace net over it, and a waist of white poplin, with turquoise velvet and chiffon and cream lace over a satin yoke. The other is woolen and of a very pretty green. The waist is trimmed with pink and green brocaded velvet and white lace, I think, and has double reefers on the front, tucked and trimmed with velvet, and also a row of tiny white buttons. Teacher, too, has a silk dress. The skirt is black, while the waist is mostly yellow, trimmed with delicate lavender chiffon and black velvet bows and lace. Her other dress is purple, trimmed with purple velvet, and the waist has a collar of cream lace. So you may imagine that we look quite like peacocks, only we have no trains."

For Annie and Helen, however, life at Red Farm was not all good conversation, play and dressing up in fine clothes. In February, after they had recovered from the shattering experience at the Gilman school, a young man named Merton S. Keith was engaged to tutor Helen for her college entrance examinations. During the rest of the winter he came out once a week by train from Boston, twenty-five miles away. In the autumn, after a summer holiday, Annie and Helen moved into an apartment in Cambridge, and he came every day, five days a week.

Those weekly tutoring sessions at Red Farm were long —three hours and a half at a stretch. All three of the participants would be exhausted at the end. It was slow, laborious work, for Mr. Keith did not know the manual alphabet, and Teacher had to spell everything he said into Helen's hand.

The great difficulty—and it *was* a great difficulty—was with algebra and geometry. Mr. Keith found Helen's preparation in history and languages, including English, excellent, but in mathematics it was practically non-existent. The fault was partly Annie's, partly Helen's. Neither of them liked math. In fact they detested it and could see no value in it. But Helen had to pass college entrance examinations in math to get into Radcliffe. So Teacher had tried to devise means of making her pupil understand a subject which she herself did not understand. For problems in plane geometry, she worked out a system with wires and pins on a cushion. But Helen got little out of it.

All that winter at Red Farm and the following winter in Boston, Mr. Keith toiled with Helen, trying to get into her head an understanding of algebra and geometry through Teacher's tireless fingers pounding in her hand. There were almost no textbooks to help her, and those that were available were not of much use. There are several kinds of Braille, and some were printed in one kind and some in another.

In vain did patient, plodding Mr. Keith try to arouse in Helen and Teacher an appreciation of what he regarded as the beauty of pure logic in mathematics. But his persistence won out in the end, to a degree where he felt that Helen was ready to take her college entrance examinations.

During the spring while she and Helen were at Red Farm, Annie's eyes began to bother her seriously. Helen's work with Mr. Keith entailed a great deal of study, and too few textbooks in Braille were available. Helen was studying advanced Latin and Greek, which meant that Annie had to spend hours poring over Latin and Greek dictionaries looking up words for her. Nothing could have been worse for her eyes.

They finally became so bad that she went to New York to consult a specialist, who told her that if she did not have another operation, she would lose her sight completely. But Annie did not think she could afford to have an operation because of the time that would be involved, as well as the money. Eventually Mrs. Hutton sent her to a doctor in Boston who treated her eyes. They still gave her a good deal of pain and fits of nausea, but she could see better. And so she went on with her work.

On two hot days at the end of June, 1898, Helen took

her final entrance examinations for Radcliffe College. Again there was the problem of finding someone to read the questions to her. Annie was barred from the room, of course. Mr. Keith thought this was unfair, but lest there ever be any question as to Helen's having taken them and passed them fairly, she and Annie accepted the ruling without question.

It was finally decided that someone should punch the questions out for Helen in Braille, so that she could read them, and that this person should be someone who did not know her or had ever had any connection with her whatever. Eugene Vining, a new teacher at the Perkins Institution, who was a complete stranger to Helen, was selected for the job. He and Helen went to work in a small room, Helen reading the questions in Braille and typing the answers.

They got along very well until they came to algebra. Helen had studied algebra in English Braille. But Mr. Vining used another kind, American Braille. This was not discovered until just before the examinations. Mr. Vining tried to explain the difference in the notations to her, but they were by no means clear, and Helen went to her examinations with a sinking heart while Teacher worried.

Somehow she got through with them and passed. In one subject, advanced Latin, she received honors. In theory, she was now ready to enter Radcliffe any time she wanted to do so.

But new difficulties arose. To get into Radcliffe, in addition to passing her entrance examinations, she had to be accepted by the Academic Board, made up of members of the faculty.

Months went by while she and Annie waited, at Wrentham during the summer and back in Boston in the winter, where Helen took more advanced work with Mr. Keith, which she did not really need.

There was a conference with Miss Agnes Irwin, dean of Radcliffe, who tried to persuade Helen to give up the idea of taking her degree. She suggested that Helen take a few special courses in English and creative writing. But these would not lead to a diploma signed by the president of Harvard.

To Annie it did not seem so important that Helen get her diploma as it did to Helen. And some of their friends and backers thought it was foolish for her to try. No blind-deaf person had ever gone to college before, let alone trying for a diploma. Teacher pointed out some of the difficulties to her.

"You'll be competing," she said, "with some of the brightest young women in the country. They've got to be good to get into Radcliffe. And they will not be blind or deaf. You did very well at Mr. Gilman's school the first year. But Radcliffe will be more difficult. You must understand that no allowance will be made for you because of your handicap."

"Of course I understand," Helen told her. "But I think I can do it. At least I can try."

Word got out around the country that Radcliffe did not want Helen Keller. It made some people angry. And two universities tried to make amends. Cornell and the University of Chicago both invited her to come to them. But Helen turned them down. She had made up her mind that she was going to Radcliffe and receive a diploma signed by the president of Harvard University, and nobody could make her change it.

Finally she sat down at her typewriter and wrote a letter to the chairman of the Academic Board of Radcliffe College:

"Dear Sir:

"As an aid to me in determining my plans for study the coming year, I apply to you for information as to the possibility of my taking the regular course in Radcliffe College.

"Since receiving my certificate of admission to Radcliffe last July, I have been studying with a private tutor Horace, Aeschylus, French, German, Rhetoric, English History, English Literature and Criticism and English Composition.

"In college I should wish to continue most if not all of these subjects. The conditions under which I work require the presence of Miss Sullivan, who has been my teacher and companion for thirteen years, as an interpreter of oral speech and as a reader of examination papers. In college she, or possibly in some subjects someone else, would of necessity be with me in the lecture-room and at recitations. I should do all my written work on a typewriter, and if a professor could not understand my speech, I could write out my answers to his questions and hand them to him after the recitation.

"Is it possible for the College to accommodate itself to these unprecedented conditions, so as to enable me to pursue my studies at Radcliffe? I realize that the obstacles in the way of my receiving a college education are very great—to others they may seem insurmountable; but, dear Sir, a true soldier does not acknowledge defeat before the battle."

Her letter was dated May 5, 1900. More than a month later, she still had not heard from the Academic Board. In a letter to Mrs. Hutton, Helen commented on the offers from Cornell and the University of Chicago.

"But if I went to any other college," she wrote, "I am afraid it would be thought that I did not pass my examinations for Radcliffe satisfactorily."

She was finally accepted, and that fall, aged twenty, she entered Radcliffe College.

There was a lot of publicity about it, but Annie, probably from force of habit, did not mention it to Helen. A couple of days after college opened, Helen Keller was elected vice-president of the freshman class. She was very much surprised.

"I didn't think most of the girls would even know I was alive!" she told Annie.

CHAPTER XIII

RADCLIFFE

For HELEN KELLER, the day she became a student at Radcliffe College was one of the proudest and happiest days of her life. Whatever misgivings Annie Sullivan may have had were shoved into the background as she watched the radiant expression on Helen's face.

They moved into a small house in Cambridge, with an Irish maid, Bridget Crimmins, to keep house for them. Annie grew very fond of Bridget, partly for Bridget's own sake and partly because she reminded her of Maggie Carroll, who had read the lives of the saints to her when she was a child at Tewksbury.

Right at the start it became apparent that the load on Annie's eyes was going to be heavier than it had ever been before. There were practically no college textbooks printed in Braille. At great expense, Colonel Rogers, their millionaire friend, and Mr. Wade, the magazine publisher at whose home they had stayed in Pennsylvania, had some printed especially for Helen. But the process was slow, and she and Annie usually did not know far enough ahead what they would need for them to be printed in time to be of much use.

More scar tissue had formed on Annie's eyes. Her vision was so limited that she had to hold the book almost up to the tip of her nose and move her head from side to side as she read. But there was neither money nor time for an operation, she insisted, and her worried friends could do nothing with her. When college opened, the eyes had had some rest. Annie and Helen had spent the summer in a cottage by a lake at Wrentham. So Annie went doggedly about her task.

Helen started out taking French, German, history, English composition and English literature. French and German caused Annie her greatest difficulty, especially German printed in strange Gothic type. There were few foreign-language dictionaries printed in Braille. Later in her college course, Helen read Homer's *Iliad*, which is not even in classical Greek, with which she was fairly familiar, but in archaic Greek. The difference between archaic Greek and classical Greek would correspond roughly to the difference between Chaucer and Shakespeare!

A strange fact was that, after all the painful hours she spent looking up words for Helen in foreign-language dictionaries—Greek, Latin, French, German—Annie never learned a foreign language herself. She had already had to learn the German and Greek alphabets. For endless hours, for eight years, while Helen was preparing for college and in college, Annie spelled strange foreign words into Helen's palm. But none of them ever stuck to her fingers.

Helen's other subjects, especially English literature, were a delight to Annie. But the burden on her eyes was heavy. For instance, in the Elizabethan period in English literature, only the plays of Shakespeare and Spencer's *Faerie Queen* were obtainable in Braille.

As Helen advanced toward her junior and senior years, some of the subjects she took must have been heavy going for Annie—medieval Latin, for instance, and a course in philosophy under the distinguished Professor Josiah Royce. But Helen also took a course in Shakespeare under Professor George L. Kittredge, probably the most celebrated Shakespearean scholar of his day. And Shakespeare, to Annie, was a greatly loved old friend, whom she had first come to know during her school days at the Perkins Institution for the Blind.

Tired as she must have been many times—times when her fingers moved mechanically, letter by letter, while her weary mind did not take in what they were spelling—a good deal of the learning Helen was acquiring must have rubbed off on Annie. In later life, her speech and the letters she wrote indicated that she was indeed a very well-educated person.

Her days were long and crowded with work. Until near the end of Helen's sophomore year, when Annie's eyes became so bad that a part-time substitute had to be found, she attended all Helen's classes with her, spelling continuously into her hand. In classes where there were recitations, this was not too difficult. She only had to make sure that Helen understood the questions. And sometimes, when the professor could not understand Helen's guttural, muffled speech, Annie would interpret for her. Only one of Helen's instructors, William Allan Neilson, who later became president of Smith College, learned the manual alphabet so that he could communicate with her.

Classes in which the professor lectured for thirty or forty minutes were more difficult for both Helen and Annie. All the other students took notes. Helen had to carry in her memory what he was saying as Annie's flying fingers spelled it into her hand.

Some of the professors were difficult to follow. They would speak rapidly sometimes, in a monotone and indistinctly. Beyond any doubt, Annie was more proficient in the use of the manual alphabet than anyone else in the world. And she had been spelling words into Helen's hand for so many years that she seldom had to finish an ordinary word. Helen would catch on after she had spelled a couple of letters. But keeping up with those professors taxed even Annie's skill, especially when they used strange, unfamiliar words. And she would be left behind. Annie never was very good at spelling.

After classes, they faced a mountain of homework. Books, books, books and more books. Other Radcliffe girls, although the courses were tough, had time for play and occasional dating. But such things were denied Helen Keller. Homework for her meant hours and hours of concentrated attention to Annie's fingers moving in her hand. Night after night, hours after the other girls had finished their homework, had had a little recreation and were in bed, Helen and Annie toiled on.

Helen was doing remarkably well in her college work. People marveled at her. She was like an airplane, sailing serenely, smoothly, effortlessly through the sky. And Annie was the hard-working, throbbing motor, unnoticed as when you watch an aircraft high overhead. Should the motor fail, however, the plane would fall crashing to the earth.

Summer vacations provided a wonderful relief to both Helen and Annie. One summer they had Helen's mother, her sister and her young brother with them in a cottage by a lake in Wrentham. Annie loved the water, and swimming became one of her favorite sports. Like many an inexperienced swimmer, she was inclined to overestimate her prowess.

One day she and Helen and Helen's brother Phillips were swimming when Phillips suddenly grabbed Helen's hand and spelled, "I don't see Teacher!"

Terrified, Helen sent Phillips for her mother. Mrs. Keller came rushing down to the dock, and within minutes some men who had been working nearby put out in a rowboat looking for Teacher. They found her desperately trying to reach an island far out in the lake, exhausted and beginning to flounder. Seconds more, and they would have been too late. The swim she had attempted would have been a long one for even an expert. She had had a narrow escape, but the next day she was out swimming again!

One summer they spent at Halifax, Nova Scotia, where they did a great deal of sailing, which Helen thoroughly enjoyed. And there was a delightful vacation with Dr. and Mrs. Bell at their summer home on Cape Breton Island, Nova Scotia, where Helen helped Dr. Bell fly kites in an experiment he was conducting to discover the laws that would govern the motion of airships.

Annie in later years often said that the summer she and Helen spent with Dr. Bell was the happiest one she had ever had. The distinguished scientist was able to give her more confidence in herself than anyone else ever did. After she had recovered from her embarrassment at their first meeting, when he asked her what method she used in teaching Helen, and she could not answer him because she did not even know what he meant, she was always comfortable with him.

"I never really felt at ease with anyone until I met him," she once said. "I was extremely conscious of my crudeness, and because I felt this inferiority, I carried a chip on my shoulder which somebody was forever trying to snap off. Dr. Bell had a happy way of making people feel pleased with themselves."

She and Helen were about to take on a big job in addition to Helen's college work when a crisis developed with Annie's eyes. Helen had known for some time how bad those eyes were. She became so worried about them that she was almost ready to leave college.

Sometimes, Annie's fingers would spell into her hand: "I don't think you got that last paragraph. I'd better read it to you again."

And Helen would lie, saying, "Oh, yes, I did. I understood it perfectly."

But she had not. And her work suffered as a result. Finally, at Helen's insistence, Annie consulted a famous, and high-priced, eye doctor.

When she admitted that she had been reading to Helen five or six hours a day, he said, "That is sheer madness, Miss Sullivan! You must rest your eyes completely if Miss Keller is to finish her college course."

Fortunately, one of their young friends, Lenore Kinney, had learned the manual alphabet, and Annie reluctantly turned over to her some of the reading.

The new, big undertaking developed out of a course in English composition Helen was taking under Professor Charles Townsend Copeland, affectionately known to hundreds of Harvard and Radcliffe students as "Copey." In the beginning, he was not very well satisfied with Helen's themes. As much as possible she was trying to write themes exactly like those written by the other students, which meant that she was writing about a world with which, because of her blindness and deafness, she was unfamiliar.

One day he had her come to his office for a conference.

"Why don't you write about things you know about?"
he asked as Teacher spelled his words into Helen's hand.
"Write about the world as it seems to you, the world you
live in. Your childhood, for instance. That should make
good reading."

So Helen started writing the story of her life, in themes,
for Professor Copeland. He was so pleased with them that
he showed them around to some of his friends, and one
day Annie and Helen were awed by a visit from the editor
of *The Ladies' Home Journal*. He had seen Helen's
themes, and the magazine would like to publish them.
They would need some editing and expanding, of course.
The price he offered was so generous that it left Annie
and Helen dazed.

Without realizing what they were getting themselves
into, they set to work on their new task. But difficulties
arose. The editing and expanding, which the magazine
editor had mentioned so casually, involved a great deal
more work than they had anticipated. And Helen's college
work must not be neglected.

Unfortunately, *The Ladies' Home Journal* started publishing the story before work on the manuscript was completed, and the magazine, Annie and Helen were all in
a state of panic when one day Lenore Kinney brought
John Macy, a brilliant young Harvard instructor, to the
house. He took in the situation at a glance, quickly
learned the manual alphabet and went to work with
Helen on the manuscript.

The Ladies' Home Journal had not finished printing
the story when a publishing house (Doubleday) came
along with an offer to bring it out in book form.

Most of the work on the book was done by John Macy,
who also helped Helen with her college work when he
could find the time. Included in the book, in addition to

Helen's story as it appeared in the magazine, were a large number of her letters, written from the time she was a child until she was ready to enter college.

Also included were many of the letters Annie wrote to Mrs. Hopkins during the early days of Helen's education. Those letters really constituted the most important part of the book for educators, for they are the only day-by-day record of how Annie led little Helen out of her dark and silent world and set about the task of making her a normal, happy human being. Since most of the letters were later destroyed, those in the book are all that are available today. And on them is still based much of the teaching of the deaf-blind.

John Macy added a brief biography of Annie Sullivan, in which Tewksbury was not mentioned, and an account of Helen's education up to the time she entered college. The book came out on March 21, 1903, toward the end of Helen's junior year in college. Before it was published, her friend in Pennsylvania, Mr. Wade, had the entire manuscript put into Braille, so that Helen could read it and make any changes she wanted.

The book was an immediate success, although there were some adverse comments from critics who could not understand why a person who was blind and deaf could have any conception of colors and sounds, as Helen indicated she had. In the years since it was published, under the title *The Story of My Life,* the book has gone into many editions and has been translated into almost every language known to man. It is still widely circulated and read. Helen Keller has written many books, some of which were highly successful, but none of them ever attained the circulation of *The Story of My Life.*

Once during Helen's college years, an attempt was made to divert her from her course. A well-meaning busybody, whose name has long since been forgotten, thought up the idea of having Annie and Helen head up a school for the deaf-blind in the United States.

At first the idea appealed to them. Annie Sullivan always felt a strong urge to help children who were afflicted as Helen was. And, as the whole world knows, Helen Keller has devoted her life to helping the blind and the deaf. Annie and Helen, however, felt that the project should wait until Helen had finished college.

The originator of the idea thought otherwise, and she went around to all those who had contributed money for Helen's education and tried to interest them in the plan. The school was to be called the Helen Keller Home. Some of them were not favorably impressed.

Dr. Bell was opposed, he said, because running a special school for deaf-blind children would cut Annie and Helen off from contact with seeing and hearing people. He suggested that an association for the deaf-blind be formed, with Annie to train teachers to instruct deaf-blind children in their homes, as she had taught Helen.

Finally a conference was called in New York, with Helen and Annie in attendance. When they were asked about the plan, they repeated their previous statement— that Helen should finish college first.

When Mark Twain, who was representing Colonel Rogers, heard that, he said, "I don't know what the Lord's wishes are in this matter, but I do know that Colonel Rogers would not be willing to finance any of His undertakings on the recommendation of Mrs.———."

That settled it, and Annie and Helen returned happily to Radcliffe.

Ninety-six earnest young women in caps and gowns were graduated from Radcliffe College on a day in June, 1904. One of them, a tall girl with light-brown hair, received a great deal of attention. She was Helen Adams Keller, the first deaf-blind person to be graduated from college. All eyes followed her as she walked up to receive her diploma, signed by the president of Harvard University.

Nobody paid much attention to a little woman, not in cap and gown, but wearing a black dress, who sat beside her among the graduates, her fingers moving in Helen's hand.

Helen was graduated *cum laude*—with honor. The little woman in black was proud of her, but not quite satisfied. She had wanted it to be *summa cum laude*—with highest honor. And she thought it might have been had she done her job better.

CHAPTER XIV

ENTER ROMANCE

O N THE DAY HELEN KELLER was graduated from Radcliffe, she and Annie, after the commencement exercises were over, took a trolley car out to their new home in Wrentham—the first home they ever owned.

During Helen's senior year, she and Annie sold some stock which their friend "King John" Spaulding had left them and bought an abandoned farm beside a lake.

The land, long neglected, had gone back into woods. The old farmhouse, large and structurally sound, was cut up into a lot of cluttery little rooms, as farmhouses were at the time when it was built. But Annie could see possibilities in it. So carpenters, plumbers, electricians and painters went to work on it.

The carpenters knocked out some partitions, put in more and larger windows. They made a study for Helen out of two pantries and a dairy. Across the front, on the second floor, they built a long balcony, where she could get some fresh air and exercise when the weather was bad.

Workmen cleaned up the woods and laid paths, along which they strung wires from tree to tree to guide Helen so that she could go for walks by herself. Landscape gardeners took over the grounds. There were some fine old trees near the house, and the lawn sloped gently down to the lake. Shrubs were planted, and a flower garden was started for Annie, who had learned a good deal about raising flowers from Helen's mother, in Alabama.

When they finished, they had made a beautiful home for Annie and Helen—a home which Annie felt provided a suitable background for Helen. It was a larger house than they really needed. Annie would learn later how much it cost to keep it up. They had undoubtedly spent more money on it than they would have spent if they had built a new, smaller house. But it belonged to them, free of debt, even though they would later feel the loss of income from the stocks they had sold.

From the beginning, the big white house was filled with guests. Helen's mother, sister and brother came for the summer. So did Mrs. Hopkins, who had befriended Annie during her school days. As she looked about at all the splendor, Mrs. Hopkins could think of only one thing to say: "Oh, my! Oh, my!"

Another guest who came for long visits was John Hitz, the gentle old Swiss man who was Dr. Bell's secretary. Annie and Helen both loved him dearly. He and Helen would take long walks together—Helen, so tall, slender and erect, Mr. Hitz, with his flowing white beard, quaint clothes and bulging pockets, spelling German into her hand.

There were other guests, who came for shorter visits or only to dine—the Chamberlins and their friends, young members of the Harvard faculty Helen and Annie had come to know. Annie Sullivan had become a famous cook, having learned from Mrs. Keller's cook in Alabama how to prepare a number of delicious Southern dishes. The house was filled with laughter and gay, witty conversation. And Annie, entertaining her guests, cooking special dishes for them and working in her flower garden, was completely happy. Her eyes, relieved of their heavy burden, no longer bothered her so much as they had while Helen was in college. She was able even to read for pleasure a little.

Other visitors came, uninvited. Groups of tourists, who wanted to see where and how Helen Keller lived. They brought picnic lunches, littered the lawn sometimes and trampled on the flower beds. But Annie put up with them with what grace she could muster. They were the price of fame, and Helen Keller, graduated *cum laude* from Radcliffe College, was one of the wonders of the world.

As might be expected, fantastic stories were circulated about her home. One Swedish newspaper carried a story that the money for the house and grounds had been raised by national subscription and given to Helen along with an annual pension of two thousand dollars for the rest of her life. A French newspaper stated that "Boston, the most intellectual city, the Athens of America," had presented Helen with the house, "in homage to the young girl who had won a victory without parallel of the spirit over matter, of the immortal soul over the senses."

One of the guests who came most often was John Macy, the young Harvard instructor who had helped Helen with her book. For John Macy had fallen in love with Annie Sullivan.

For a year, Annie kept him dangling. She was filled with misgivings. First, there was Helen, who needed her constant care and attention—or so Annie was convinced. John would have to share her with Helen. She felt it would not be fair to him, and she could not believe that a marriage under such conditions could be made to work.

There was also the question of age. Annie was now thirty-nine. She was losing her figure, beginning to grow heavy. She still had beautiful clothes and knew how to wear them. But John was only twenty-eight, nearer Helen's age. In fact, during their courtship a story got into one of the Boston papers that it was Helen he was courting, not Annie.

Helen became involved in the arguments. One night she said to Annie, "If you love John and let him go, I shall feel like a hideous accident."

Finally Annie said, "Yes," but even after that she changed her mind so many times that John suggested that they have printed on the wedding invitations, "Subject to change without notice."

Annie and John were married on May 2, 1905, in the living room of the home in Wrentham. It was a small wedding. Members of John's family were there, Mrs. Keller, Mrs. Hopkins, Mr. Hitz, Lenore Kinney, who had read to Helen at Radcliffe when Annie's eyes gave out, and Lenore's husband, Philip Smith. They assembled at noon for lunch, which Annie had helped to prepare. She had baked the wedding cake herself.

At two o'clock they moved into the living room, where Annie and John took their places before a large window filled with flowers and ferns. There was no best man. Helen stood beside Annie, and, next to Helen, Lenore Kinney, spelling the words of the service into her hand. Helen's distant cousin, the distinguished author and clergyman, Dr. Edward Everett Hale, officiated.

It was Annie's wedding, but everybody was watching Helen and thinking about her. Even as a bride, Annie played a secondary role to her famous pupil. The following day, Dr. Hale wrote Helen a letter, in which he said:

"The tie between you and our dear Annie is as close

as any tie can possibly be. I dare say plenty of people have told you that there is nothing like it in history or literature. You do not care anything about that. You know just how much she loves you and how much you love her. Now bear in mind that love is not measured in pints or pecks. It is infinite in all its relations. And never permit yourself for an instant to think that Annie loves you less than she ever did, or that the tie to her husband can tempt her to love you less. She will love you more."

Later in his letter, Dr. Hale suggested that Helen might not need that advice. And he was right. She never resented John Macy, but welcomed him into the family as a dearly loved brother. Nor did John Macy resent Helen. They remained friends as long as he lived.

After the marriage, life in the Wrentham household went on for a time as it had before—gay, carefree, with guests in and out, a gracious way of living, which Annie Sullivan, as a little girl at Tewksbury, had dimly imagined the women in *Godey's Lady's Book* enjoyed.

Some decision had to be made about Helen's future, however. It had always been her intention to support herself after she finished college. Otherwise, she thought, there would have been no use in her going to college. At one time she thought of doing settlement work.

Not long after Helen finished college, she received a letter from Andrew Carnegie, the steel magnate, offering her a pension of five thousand dollars a year for life. But Helen wrote him a polite letter turning it down.

"I intend to earn my living," she proudly announced.

To Annie and to John Macy, it was perfectly apparent that the way for Helen to support herself was by writing. Annie, now that Helen had won her degree, felt that the four years in college had been largely wasted, except that

Helen had proved to her own satisfaction and to the world that she could do it. But she never told Helen that.

John Macy had left his teaching job at Harvard to become associate editor of *The Youth's Companion*. He was also having considerable success as a critic and essayist. With his help, Helen Keller set out to become a professional writer.

Her next book, *The World I Live In,* was accepted and published immediately. In it she tried to answer the critics who had said she did not know what she was talking about when she described colors and sounds in *The Story of My Life*. She wrote a long poem, *The Song of the Stone Wall,* in which she described her satisfaction in helping to build a stone wall on the place at Wrentham. For *The Ladies' Home Journal, The Youth's Companion* and other magazines, she wrote articles about the blind.

It was apparent that she would have no trouble finding publishers for whatever she wrote about herself or the blind. But a time came when she felt written out on those subjects.

Looking around for new material, she began to write about controversial subjects, to espouse unpopular causes. Her first difficulty arose out of an article she submitted to the *Century Magazine* on the controversy, causing a lot more heat then than it could today, as to who wrote Shakespeare's plays, William Shakespeare or Sir Francis Bacon. Helen was on the side of Sir Francis Bacon. Her old friend, Richard Watson Gilder, editor of the magazine, turned the article down and blamed the Macys for leading her astray. Actually, neither John nor Annie had any strong feelings on the subject. It was Helen's own thinking.

Mark Twain agreed with Helen, but wrote her that it was useless to try to convince anyone.

"Such labors are not worth the ink and the paper," he assured her, "except that you do them for the pleasure of it. Shakespeare, the Stratford tradesman, will still be the divine Shakespeare to our posterity a thousand years hence."

The Shakespeare-Bacon article was not published, so there was no public reaction to it. But when Helen Keller wrote an article for *The Ladies' Home Journal* on the prevention of blindness in newborn babies whose parents had venereal disease, the public was shocked. This was not a subject to be discussed by that "dear, sweet little wonder child." And when she backed such unpopular causes as woman suffrage and labor unions, she lost her market completely. Neither editors nor the public would accept the fact that Helen Keller had grown up, that she was an adult with ideas of her own and the right to express them.

Nobody, of course, blamed the "wonder child" for going astray. They blamed the Macys, especially Annie. Annie by no means shared Helen's fervor for remaking the world. Tewksbury—about which she still kept silent—had taught her long ago that there were many people in the world who, through no fault of their own, were destined to live in misery and want. Life was like that.

She did not even rage inwardly, as Helen did, at some of the strange contrasts that confronted them. One night they might be dining in a luxurious home with some of their wealthy friends. The following night might find them answering a distress call to the home of a working-man who had been blinded that day in an industrial accident, and whose wife was wondering how she was going to house, feed and clothe their children without his wages. Such things made a socialist out of Helen. They made Annie unhappy.

Annie did not agree with many of Helen's ideas. But she had spent her life developing Helen Keller as an independent personality, with a mind of her own. She certainly was not going to interfere with her now!

Even as Helen lost her market as a writer, however, her prestige with the public remained high. She had been misled into making mistakes by her teacher, people told themselves, but she was still Helen Keller, and she was supposed to know everything there was to know about the blind.

Helen's mail had always been heavy. During the years at Wrentham, it kept increasing until the volume became so great that even the combined efforts of Helen herself and the Macys could hardly cope with it. There would be appeals for sympathy and money, which neither Helen nor Annie had the heart to refuse. Blind college students would write to Helen for advice—and inspiration. Societies, well-meaning individuals and worried, unhappy mothers would ask her how to handle blind children. Sometimes the questions would involve research, for, contrary to the common belief, Helen was by no means an infallible authority on blindness. Research meant work for the Macys, who would have to search out material and read it to her.

Nobody ever thought of asking Annie's advice, although Annie knew more about how to raise and educate a handicapped child than Helen did. It was always Helen they sought after, Helen's advice they wanted. Annie only punished her eyes looking up material for Helen and answering letters for Helen to sign!

In 1906, two years after she finished college, Helen was appointed to the Massachusetts Commission for the Blind.

"I could have wished," she wrote the governor of Massachusetts, "that you had appointed in my stead my teacher, Mrs. Macy, whose long experience gives her unique qualifications in all work for the blind. What reconciles me is the fact, which you doubtless took into account, that she must always be at my side to give me the benefit of her wisdom."

CHAPTER XV

WANDERERS

THERE WERE a few happy, carefree years at Wrentham —four or five in all—before it became apparent that Helen Keller was not going to be able to earn her living as a professional writer.

The situation was complicated by the fact that through her earnings, she must also support her teacher. So long as she remained constantly at Helen's side, Annie had no way of earning money independently from Helen. In the past she had received some tempting offers, but these were no longer forthcoming. And anyway, to leave Helen was unthinkable.

By 1912, eight years after Helen finished college, she and Annie were having a hard time making ends meet. Before her marriage, Annie, who was as innocent about business affairs as a baby, had made a disastrous investment in a coal mine that never amounted to anything. This, with the loss of income from the stocks they had sold to build their home, had reduced their financial backlog almost to the vanishing point. They had nothing except the diminishing royalties from Helen's books. The house at Wrentham was expensive to keep up, and the demands on Helen to help the needy blind were heavy. They had reached the point where they had to look to John for help, and the income he received from his books and articles, brilliant and scholarly though they were, was not large.

Annie was not well. She worried constantly over their financial situation, the cost of keeping up their home, their dependence on John. And always she carried a heavy load of work, trying to keep up with Helen's mail, working to improve her speech. The housework had become a burden to her.

At that time there appeared to be some possibility of doing something about Helen's speech. Three years earlier, in 1909, she had met Charles White, of the Boston Conservatory of Music. Mr. White believevd that the monotonous, guttural tones she produced could be changed into something more normal, and he started giving her voice lessons, without pay. For three years he worked with her. In the end there was some slight improvement, but Helen Keller's voice would always remain flat and dull, without inflection, and her words so muffled that it was difficult for strangers to understand her.

Those voice lessons were extremely important to Helen, for in the back of her mind she had an idea. Since she could not earn her living as a writer, she could think of only one possible way of supporting herself and Teacher. This would be by paid lectures if her speech improved as much as she hoped it would. If it did not—and as it turned out, she was disappointed—the only way she could lecture would be with Teacher at her side to interpret for her. For a long time she did not mention her idea to Annie.

In September, 1912, matters in the household at Wrentham reached a crisis. Annie was taken to a hospital for a major operation. She was critically ill, and the outcome was uncertain. John, who had taken a job as secretary to the mayor of Schenectady, New York, resigned and returned home to be with her. And Helen, frantic with worry and desperately lonely, was sent to Washington to stay with Lenore Kinney and her husband.

In three weeks Annie was back home, her condition somewhat improved, but the doctors told her she would have to take a long rest and be careful for at least a year.

By this time, with hospital and doctors' bills to be paid, the situation was so bad that something had to be done about it—and quickly. Helen told Annie about her plan.

Helen had received an offer to make a paid lecture in Montclair, New Jersey. She had received such offers many times before, but she and Annie had always rejected them as impossible. Annie had been out of the hospital for less than four months when she and Helen went to Montclair for Helen's first paid lecture.

It was a most trying experience for both of them. Helen spoke for a few minutes about what it was like to be blind and deaf and made a plea for help for others handicapped as she was. Annie interpreted for her, sentence by sentence, and then gave a talk of her own, describing Helen's accomplishments and how she had achieved them. Helen left the stage in tears, thinking she had made a miserable failure, and Annie felt like weeping herself as she tried to comfort her.

To their astonishment, however, they were called back to the stage for several curtain calls. The audience loved them! Newspaper accounts of their performance were friendly and complimentary. The result was that Helen accepted several offers to lecture for pay the following spring.

Traveling was not easy for either Helen or Annie. Annie's eyes suffered horribly as she pored over the fine print in railroad time tables, and half the time she would get them mixed up. Handling money was difficult for her, and more than once she gave enormous tips because she had not distinguished a five-dollar bill from a one-dollar bill. Guiding Helen around the streets in strange cities was torture. She would hesitate for a long time on curbs, looking in both directions, and even then vehicles would sometimes come bearing down on them from nowhere.

Helen, in a different hotel every night, was completely lost. To move about freely and with confidence, as she did in her own home, she had to know exactly where everything was. In a strange hotel room, she had to find her way about, running into furniture, stumbling over things. If someone carelessly moved any of her belongings —her Braille slate, for instance—it could take her hours to find it. When Annie was not with her, she could only sit, helpless and completely alone.

But the lectures were highly successful, and somehow the two of them managed until one dreadful April night in Bath, Maine. Annie had a bad cold, which kept getting worse, and after the lecture that night she could barely drag herself and Helen back to their hotel. The cold had developed into a severe case of influenza, and during the night her temperature skyrocketed, and she became delirious.

Helen could do nothing except sit by her bed, gripping her hand, from which she got no response. Even if she could have found the telephone—and she did not dare leave Annie's side—she would have been unable to make herself understood. For her to find her way through a maze of hotel corridors and down to the desk clerk in the lobby was impossible.

Finally, in the morning, Annie roused herself enough to reach the telephone and call for help. Several days later two weary, frightened women made their way back to Wrentham. Never again did they try to go on a trip alone. And Helen swallowed her pride and wrote to Andrew Carnegie, accepting his proffered pension.

A few weeks later, in May, 1913, John Macy sailed for Europe. It was the beginning of a rift between Annie and John that would widen and become permanent. All three of them—Annie, John and Helen—would always remain reticent about the break. Both Annie and John insisted that Helen was in no way involved, and years later, long after the rift had become permanent, Annie, who was ill, begged Helen to turn to John for help if she did not recover. There was never a divorce, and he sometimes came to see them long after they had left Wrentham.

Money was needed, and so in the autumn of 1913, only a few months after that bad night in Bath, Maine, Annie and Helen accepted an offer from the Pond Lecture Bureau and again took to the road. But this time they were not alone. Helen's mother went with them on this and several succeeding trips, to Annie's enormous relief.

From the beginning, the lectures were tremendously successful. In Washington, Helen was introduced to the audience by Dr. Bell and in New Haven, Connecticut, by former President William Howard Taft, who was then teaching at Yale University. On that trip, Annie and Helen met Thomas A. Edison, Henry Ford and the great tenor, Enrico Caruso. The audiences were large and enthusiastic, and the lecture bureau was delighted. In January, 1914, Annie, Helen and Mrs. Keller set out on another trip, all the way across the United States and up into Canada.

They had their program for the audiences well worked

out by this time. Helen would talk for fifteen or twenty minutes, Annie translating what she said, sentence by sentence. At the end of fifteen or twenty minutes, the audience would begin to grow tired and restless because of the strain of trying to follow Helen. Then Annie would take over. This meant that Annie would fill a greater part of the program than Helen did, but people who would never have bought tickets to see and hear Annie alone listened with interest.

Annie talked about Helen, of course. Over and over, night after night, she assured them that Helen Keller was no genius, that she had worked hard for everything she had achieved. People didn't want to hear that, and they didn't believe her. Helen Keller, to them, was the "wonder child" grown up. It was impossible for them to think of her any other way.

Annie also talked about her theories of education. She thought it was a mistake to try to fit every child into a mold and to try to force him to learn things for which he had no aptitude or interest.

"But freedom," she would say, "does not mean that he should be allowed to grow like a weed or a barbarian. Nothing worth while is ever got without effort. I am thoroughly convinced that the child must not have forced upon him things he is not interested in because he is not ready for them. I am equally certain that learning must not be merely haphazard play. He must not nibble the sweets and leave out the substance.

"There must be coherence and an effective process of stimulating his pleasure in a given subject until he has gained the mental discipline necessary to pursue it further. Joyous freedom must be wedded to accuracy and clear understanding, through which come self-discipline and self-control. The teacher must not let him scatter his efforts, his will and his curiosity by studying in a careless, inattentive manner. The true function of the teacher is to keep him interested."

One of the most celebrated teachers of that period was the Italian Madame Montessori, regarded as a pioneer both in modern education and for her work with defective children. She and Annie were on the platform together at a meeting of educators in San Francisco in the summer of 1915.

"I have been called a pioneer," Madame Montessori said, "but there"—pointing dramatically at Annie—"is your pioneer!"

Back and forth up and down the country they traveled all through the late winter and spring of 1914—Annie, Helen and Mrs. Keller. Some of their trips were badly planned. They would find themselves riding all night in a day coach, arriving in some town at dawn, with nobody to meet them. One strange hotel after another, some of them uncomfortable and dirty. Tiresome banquets, with the same poorly cooked chicken, carrots and peas, lettuce dressed with vinegar and little oil, tasteless brick ice cream, the dishes that were supposed to be hot more than half cold, the ice cream melting as much as it could with all the gelatin it contained. Always there were reporters, many of them with stupid, prying questions, and photographers with flashlights. In those days, photographers did not use bulbs as they do now. They exploded black powder in a little metal trough, with a deafening bang and a lot of smoke.

Helen worried about Annie's health. In a letter she wrote:

"I really wonder how Teacher is able to go on. She is very, very tired, although she will NOT admit it. At times she trembles so much that we marvel when she gets through the lecture, and nothing happens."

They were in Buffalo in May when Annie did not see a short flight of stairs, fell and broke her arm at the elbow. Her vision had become so poor that she needed to be guided almost as much as Helen did. She also had high blood pressure and frequent colds that left her with a cough.

From Buffalo, Mrs. Keller accompanied them back to Wrentham and left them there, two lonely women in a big house that seemed unbearably empty. For company they had only Thora, Helen's great Dane. Annie, with her fondness for dogs, treated Thora as though she were a human being.

Late that summer, Polly Thomson entered their lives, one of the rarest pieces of good fortune they would ever know. Because of the money they made on the lecture tours, their financial situation had eased somewhat, and they looked around for a secretary. Mrs. Keller, no longer young, could not go on traveling with them forever. She made her home with Helen's sister, Mildred, who was married and living in Montgomery, Alabama.

Polly's home was in Scotland, and she had come over to visit some relatives near Boston, when somebody brought her to see Annie and Helen. Polly was in her twenties and had taken a secretarial course in Scotland. She was sturdy and practical, with a sense of humor and a Scottish burr that won Annie's heart immediately. She had heard of Helen Keller, but knew little about her and had never had any association with the blind or the deaf. But she took the job and in a thoroughly businesslike manner set about learning the manual alphabet and straightening out Annie's and Helen's checkbooks, which had not been balanced in years. Her "visit" to the United

States was to last for more than forty years. For she stayed on with Helen and traveled all over the world with her after Teacher died, until her own death in 1960.

Polly came to Annie and Helen a few months after the outbreak of World War I in Europe. Annie thought there might not be any more demand for the lectures because of the war, but the Pond Lecture Bureau thought otherwise, and the trips continued, with Polly's keen brown eyes guiding Annie and Helen through traffic, reading time tables, watching over their money and doing a thousand and one things to make them comfortable and happy.

"How did we ever get along without her?" Annie used to ask Helen.

The lectures were successful, both financially and in the continuous ovations they brought to Helen. But by late 1915, Annie and Helen had become so interested and so involved in public issues that they could no longer bring themselves to go traveling about the country talking about education and the needs of the blind.

Helen was heart and soul in the woman suffrage movement. Annie did not go along with her on that. But they were both passionately concerned with efforts to stop the war. Helen, with Annie at her side, made two speeches in New York that labeled her as a pacifist. The audiences were large and enthusiastic. But the newspapers ripped her to pieces.

The following summer, 1916, Annie and Helen went out for a few weeks on the Chautauqua circuit, talking against war. The trip was a miserable, humiliating failure. By the summer of 1916, the American people were beginning to wake up to the danger of the war spreading from Europe over here.

Annie returned to Wrentham obviously a sick woman.

The cough that had never really left her had become much worse. It racked her whole body. And she had sharp pains in her side.

The doctor at Wrentham told her to go immediately to Lake Placid, New York. He may not have known that Annie's mother and her brother Jimmie had died of tuberculosis, since Annie still maintained secrecy about her childhood. But Annie knew.

CHAPTER XVI

WINTER IN THE SUN

ANNIE AND POLLY THOMSON took a night train to Lake
Placid on November 20, 1916. Helen and her mother,
who had come up from Alabama to look after her, saw
them off. The following morning Helen wrote to her
teacher:

"I don't know how I stood the pain of having you go
last night. As we walked to the car I felt suddenly over-
whelmed with loneliness and nameless dread. It seemed
as if some grim destiny would take you from me forever."

It may not have been a very wise letter to write to
Annie at that moment, but it came from the heart.

The doctors at Lake Placid diagnosed the case as the
doctor at Wrentham had expected. They took X-rays of
Annie's chest and told her she had tuberculosis.

The area surrounding Lake Placid in the Adirondacks
was at that time, next to Switzerland, probably the world's
leading center for the treatment of tuberculosis. There
were hospitals everywhere, filled with tuberculosis patients.

The prescribed treatment put the patient to bed for

months, and in the daytime the bed would be wheeled out onto a terrace, even in the biting winter cold. The cure was supposed to result from prolonged inactivity, nourishing food, sunshine and fresh air. There were no drugs available for treatment of the disease such as those used in recent years with some success, and the regimen imposed on patients was long and dull.

Annie was fifty years old when she went to Lake Placid. Although she could drive herself to lengths almost beyond human endurance for Helen, it was next to impossible for her to accept discipline from others—not even from doctors who were trying to save her life. She hated the cold, the other patients bored her, she was as unmanageable as she had been during her first years at the Perkins school. And she was utterly miserable. In her letters, Polly told Helen, and Helen tried her best to cheer Annie up.

"I am grieved," she wrote, "to hear from Polly that you find it so depressing at Lake Placid. I don't wonder that you do, with such a trying combination of bad weather, medical bugbears, 'elderly, stodgy people,' and loneliness, and the worn-out feeling you speak of. But wait a little, and the splendid, silent sun shall pour its sweet balm upon you. Then perhaps the still, small voice in your heart will whisper a message of peace that you can hear amid the silent glory of the snow-robed mountains."

Helen had gone with her mother to Montgomery, Alabama, to spend the winter with her sister, Mildred.

"And there is a chance," she added, "of your spending Christmas here. We shall look for you and look awfully hard."

But nothing that the doctors or Polly could say and not even the prospect of being permitted to spend Christmas with Helen in Alabama had much effect. Annie Sullivan had always been a rebel, except where Helen was concerned. She could not resign herself to a winter in bed on a balcony surrounded by icy, snow-capped mountains.

One Sunday a small advertisement in the *New York Times* caught her attention. It contained a tiny picture of a beach in Puerto Rico, with palms in the background. It described the climate in Puerto Rico as "soft as June." In Puerto Rico there would be flowers, beauty, romance.

When Polly came to see her during visiting hours she announced, "Polly, we are going to Puerto Rico."

There was a special cruise ship leaving for Puerto Rico every Saturday from New York. But Annie did not wait for it. She and Polly sailed on another ship the following Wednesday.

"It was an eleven days' sail," she wrote Helen from San Juan, "out of the snow, the piercing winds and the leaden skies of the Adirondacks into the sunshine of the southern seas. It seemed incredible, Helen! I had to pinch myself to see if I was awake or dreaming. There, beyond that narrow stretch of rippling, sun-warmed ocean, was Puerto Rico, like a great ship afloat in violet waters!"

Thus began the longest period of separation between Helen Keller and Annie Sullivan as long as they both lived. It lasted four months, from late November, 1916, until early April, 1917, shortly after the United States entered World War I.

As always, with Annie and Helen, there were financial problems. They had made money on their lecture trips, but they had spent most of it. Helen later wrote that without Andrew Carnegie's five-thousand-dollar pension, the winter for Annie in Puerto Rico would have been impossible. That was the only time she ever hinted that there might have been a shortage of funds, either in her letters to Annie or in a book she wrote about her years later.

All that winter, Annie in her letters begged Helen to bring her mother and join her in Puerto Rico. Helen gave as her reason for not going her belief that Annie needed to be away from her, for a complete rest. She never mentioned money.

If Annie Sullivan had a dollar in her purse, she could not help spending it. She was like that all her life. But if Helen felt any dismay when Annie wrote her that she had had a chauffeur bring their car to Puerto Rico, she gave no sign of it. She was only happy that Annie had the car so that she could get out and take trips about the island. The only thing that mattered to her was that Annie get well. Since she was living with her family in Montgomery, she was undoubtedly able to keep her own expenses down.

She did write Annie that, after she was well, they might live more simply than they had in the past.

"I do think," she wrote, "that when you are better, we must start our life over again, reducing it to the simplest terms possible. (Of course the simple life does not exclude a few modern conveniences, or machinery that turns drudgery into joyous activity.) We can travel more as we like without lecturing, and we can see more of our friends. We can bring about this change anywhere—in Wrentham, or Puerto Rico, or the Sandwich Islands. All we need is courage to do the sensible thing. Don't you dare tell me it's too late!"

For fifteen dollars a month, Annie and Polly rented a four-room cottage, which in their letters they referred to as "the shack," high in the hills away from San Juan. It was set in a grove of orange and grapefruit trees, with a pineapple patch in front of it. It had no glass windows;

houses in Puerto Rico have only shutters, to be closed when the hurricanes come. If it had any doors, they were wide open, for Annie wrote Helen a humorous account of oxen marching solemnly into her room and gazing at her "with deep pools of quiet in their eyes" while the little Puerto Rican dog she had adopted barked furiously.

All that winter there was a continuous stream of letters back and forth between Annie and Helen. Helen wrote on her typewriter. Although Annie's vision continued slowly and steadily to deteriorate, she was still able to read. But Annie had not used Braille for thirty years. She had always detested it and was never very good at it. She had even forgotten the Braille alphabet, and Helen had to send her a copy.

Her letters to Helen that winter were a labor of love, for, as she said, punching out Braille for her was "like trying to punch a hole in the universe with a toe." But slowly and laboriously, with a stiletto that always felt awkward in her hand, she pricked out long, beautifully composed letters to Helen. Not since the days when she wrote weekly letters to Mrs. Hopkins, during the first months after she had become Helen's teacher, had Annie Sullivan written so many letters. She could have used abbreviations, sloppy short cuts, but she never did. Every sentence was rounded out, complete, and many of the descriptions of her beloved Puerto Rico were vivid and beautiful.

"The island is a dream of loveliness," she wrote, "a perfect riot of color, blooming trees and shrubs, roses, clematis, tree-like lilies, poinsettias and many beautiful flowers I never saw before. But best of all, the climate is glorious, warm, not hot. I mean it is not cruelly hot. There is always a delightful breeze from the ocean. The houses are painted all colors of the rainbow."

She and Polly, neither of whom spoke Spanish, had great fun making themselves understood by the Puerto Ricans, she said:

"No matter what we say, they always answer, 'Si.' That means yes. They look bewildered when we shake our heads. The sign language is our chief means of communication."

In another letter she reminded Helen that John Bunyan had gone to jail rather than attend the parish church.

"And I'll be martyred somehow," she added, "before I'll return to the Adirondacks.

"I'm glad I didn't inherit the New England conscience. If I did, I should be worrying about the state of sin I am now enjoying in Puerto Rico. One can't help being happy here, Helen—happy and idle and aimless and pagan —all the sins we are warned against. I go to bed every night soaked with sunshine and orange blossoms and fall to sleep to the soporific sound of oxen munching banana leaves.

"We sit on the porch every evening and watch the sunset melt from one vivid color to another—rose, asphodel (Do you know what color that is? I thought it was blue, but I have learned that it is golden yellow) to violet, then deep purple. Polly and I hold our breath as the stars come out in the sky—they hang low in the heavens like lamps of many colors—and myriads of fireflies come out on the grass and twinkle in the dark trees."

Having predicted, soon after her arrival in Puerto Rico, that it would be some time before she would be good for much, Annie seldom mentioned her health. But Polly kept Helen informed. Teacher was better, but she was still a long way from being well. Helen must have shown some concern, for Annie wrote her:

"Helen, you must not worry about the future. I am not

going to die yet—I know that I am going to get well. I don't feel ill a bit. In fact, if it weren't for that horrid laboratory report, I shouldn't know there was anything wrong with me."

But in another letter, she wrote:

"You are never out of my thoughts. They keep me awake at night, and daylight brings no satisfactory answers to them. When I married John I thought I had solved the greatest of them. He promised that, in case of my death, which in the natural course would come before his, he would be a brother to you, look after your happiness and take charge of your affairs. For years my mind was at rest on this—to you and me—most important of matters. But ever since he left us I have worried.

"He seemed and still seems the only one to take care of you when I go. Perhaps, dear, it would be best all round to let him do what he can to make things a little easier for you when I am gone. He understands your business better than anyone else. And would it not be better in every way to let the suffering, the unhappiness that has come to all three of us die with me?"

Important events in world history were taking place that winter as the United States moved closer and closer to war with Germany. But Annie was almost as remote from them as though she were at the South Pole. She never saw any newspapers except when she and Polly went to San Juan, and then they would be several days old. She did not even have a calendar; all her letters to Helen were undated. She and Helen were still just as strongly opposed to the war and to our entrance into it as they had ever been. But while Helen fumed and fretted in Montgomery, Alabama, Annie contentedly soaked up sunshine and beauty in Puerto Rico. Nothing, except Helen's welfare and future, seemed to matter to her very much. Never before in

her life—not even during the happy years at Wrentham—
had she been so completely relaxed and carefree.

Annie had announced when she went to Puerto Rico
that she would remain there until April. And when April
finally came, she and Polly, with their chauffeur and car,
sailed for New York, where Helen and her mother met
them. A few days earlier, the United States had declared
war on Germany.

They went first to Wrentham, to dismantle their home
and put it up for sale. Much as they loved it, the big
house had long been a financial burden. Now, with prices
going up on account of the war, they could hold onto it no
longer. A big department store bought it and turned it
into a rest home for girls.

The wrench of giving up their home took its toll from
Annie. She was far from well when they rented a cottage
by a lake in Vermont. By autumn she was feeling much
better. So she decided to go back to Lake Placid for a
check-up.

A very much embarrassed doctor told her, "This is one
of those things that are supposed never to happen. Your
charts got mixed up with the charts belonging to someone
else. I am very happy to tell you, though, that you do not
have tuberculosis. You have never had tuberculosis."

The joy which Helen and Polly experienced over the
good news was not fully shared by Annie. She was constantly bothered by her failing eyesight, which made her
move awkwardly and with a good deal of effort. She still
tired quickly and felt far from well.

With the United States at war and with everything in a
turmoil, it was impossible for Annie and Helen to think
seriously of settling down in some remote place—Puerto
Rico, the Sandwich Islands or even California. Helen still

hoped that she might use whatever influence she had to help end the war. So they went to New York.

They stayed temporarily in a small, inconspicuous hotel, looking about for a place to live. The headwaiter in the dining room told them he knew of a house for sale in Forest Hills, a suburb of New York. So they went out to look at it.

It was a small, ugly house in a poor neighborhood. But the price was within their means, so they bought it and set to work improving it as much as they could. There was a lot of "gingerbread" on it, and this they had removed. Ugly stained-glass windows were replaced. The attic was converted into a study for Helen. And in the small, cramped garden, a row of evergreens was planted, so that Helen could walk back and forth behind them to get exercise.

Teacher could no longer see well enough to take her for long walks through the streets, and Polly, loaded down with secretarial work and household chores, could rarely find the time.

CHAPTER XVII

HOLLYWOOD ADVENTURE

As ANNIE AND HELEN settled themselves, with Polly and a beautiful fawn-colored great Dane, Sieglinde, in their new home in Forest Hills, their financial problems were still with them.

Andrew Carnegie's five-thousand-dollar annual pension could have supported them comfortably those days if they had spent it carefully and had no extra expenses. But they had extra expenses, some of them essential, most of them due to their inability to refuse pleas for help and to Annie's incurable urge to spend money when she had it, without thought of the future.

Polly Thomson was essential. She was supposed to receive a salary, and when Annie and Helen had the money she did. When they did not, she worked without pay. When they could afford it, they had a maid, and Polly devoted herself to being a secretary and trying to keep their finances in order. When they could not afford a maid, Polly cooked and scrubbed and washed for them.

In her role as housekeeper when they needed one, Polly was even more essential than she was as a secretary. Annie's vision was so bad that she could no longer do much about the house. Helen had long ago learned to wash dishes and make beds, but naturally she could not cook or scrub or wash clothes. Seemingly, there was nothing Polly Thomson could not do.

Even with their reduced scale of living in the ugly little house in Forest Hills, Helen's pension could not cover everything. And since whatever they earned would depend on her, she desperately tried to think of a way to earn some money.

Her worry was deeper than that imposed by their present situation. It was a matter that had troubled her for some time, especially during those long, lonely months in Alabama while Teacher was in Puerto Rico. She knew that if she herself should die, Mr. Carnegie's pension would die with her. And then what would become of Teacher, getting old, in poor health, gradually going blind—and penniless? Helen's one ambition in life at that point was to find a way of earning enough money so that she could lay some away for Teacher.

Lecturing, as they had done it in the past, seemed to be out of the question. The United States was at war; people were deeply engrossed in a gigantic effort to win that war. Nobody was interested in hearing what Helen Keller had to say about the blind, or in anything else she had to say, for that matter. Least of all was the American public interested in what she had to say about the subject nearest to her heart, to find some way to end the war.

Briefly, Annie and Helen considered the possibility of going overseas to work with blind soldiers in the military hospitals. But the idea was hardly worth considering at all. They were both so handicapped that they would have been a burden to the military authorities, rather than a help. And Helen's reputation as a pacifist would very likely have made her unacceptable, anyway.

They were still working away, getting their new home in order, while Helen worried, when seemingly a kind providence dropped a plum into Helen's lap. The plum was an offer to make a motion picture of Helen Keller's life.

It started with a visit early in 1918 from Dr. Francis Trevelyn Miller, who was writing a history of the world. He had had an inspiration, he said. A motion picture based on the life of Helen Keller and her long, heroic struggle through darkness and silence to achieve all that she had done might bring people to their senses, might inspire them to look for a way to peace instead of continuing the bloody struggle in the trenches. Naturally, Annie and Helen were very much interested.

Dr. Miller's idea was that money to finance the film might be raised by voluntary contributions from the public. But his idea was rejected by Annie. It would be impossible, she said, to raise the money that way.

They were about to abandon the idea when a widely known multimillionaire financier—whose name, at his own request, was never revealed—offered to finance the project. In high spirits, Annie and Helen and Polly, naively convinced that they were about to become rich, set out for Hollywood. The money advanced by the financier was a very large sum, and for the next few months they lived like queens.

The undertaking ran into snags from the start. Before they left New York, Miss Elisabeth Marbury, one of the most famous theatrical agents of her day, predicted ominously that a commercially successful motion picture could not be made out of Helen Keller's life.

"After the scene at the pump and Helen's release, what

do you have?" she demanded. "Nothing. No love interest. No drama. Nothing. Whatever happened—and what happened, I'll grant you, is magnificent and wonderful—happened inside Helen's head. You can't dramatize that. If you want a successful movie, you'll have to make up the rest of the story. It will have to be fiction."

This suggestion made Annie and Helen furious. If a motion picture was to be made, they insisted, it must be absolutely truthful. No fiction. No distortion of facts.

In Hollywood, the red carpet was rolled out for them literally. They were taken everywhere, met all the movie celebrities, including Mary Pickford, Douglas Fairbanks and Charlie Chaplin. They lived sumptuously, in a wonderful outdoor setting. One of the first things they did was to take up horseback riding—all three of them, with a groom for Helen. That entailed the purchase of expensive riding clothes. But they had plenty of money for once in their lives, no financial worries. Of course they might have laid some money aside for future use. But they did not. After all, they were going to be rich!

A child was engaged to take Helen's part in the early scenes, and young actresses were hired for the roles of the youthful Annie Sullivan and Helen Keller during her college days. The director was George Platt, highly regarded for his successful stage production of Maeterlinck's *Bluebird*.

Production ran into trouble almost immediately because there were three different ideas as to what the picture should be. Annie and Dr. Miller insisted that it be a true historical record. Mr. Platt wanted it to be an artistic triumph. The financier, apparently thinking of Helen's financial interest, did not care what they did with it so long as it was a big commercial success. And nobody had complete authority.

The early scenes came off, as expected, with no difficulty. Everyone around the studio was thrilled. The scenes were beautiful and very moving. The scene where Helen spoke her first words, "I am not dumb now," was tremendously affecting.

But when they started getting into Helen's adult life, they ran into trouble, as Miss Marbury had predicted they would. They tried to develop a subplot, with love interest in it, but that did not work. Mr. Platt, apparently under the influence of Maeterlinck, worked out some elaborate symbolic scenes.

In one of them, Knowledge, represented by a beautiful maiden, wrestled with a monster, Ignorance, at the entrance to the cave of Father Time for the soul of the infant Helen Keller. Then Helen, grown to womanhood and played by herself, appeared as the Mother of Sorrows before a large group of Hollywood extras representing suffering humanity. One scene had Helen galloping off somewhere on a white horse, blowing a trumpet and leading the world to deliverance. Helen named the picture. She called it *Deliverance*.

In the midst of all the difficulties, Helen surprised everybody by proving to be a really good actress, in spite of the weird things she was asked to do. Annie worked out a system of taps by which directions could be relayed to Helen as she or Polly pounded them out on the floor. Tough Hollywood movie people had tears in their eyes as they watched her. Nobody believed the picture could possibly be a failure. It was going to be a smash hit. It had to be!

At the studio, the film was still being cut and put together when Annie and Helen and Polly left Hollywood. They had to leave because they had run out of money and could not ask for more. In fact, they had to borrow money to get home. But they were not downhearted or worried. Riches lay ahead of them. They were sure of that.

They arrived home on the day after Christmas, 1918, to a little house that looked not only ugly to them, after the luxury in which they had been living, but neglected and dirty. They had no more money, so Polly cleaned it up. And they settled down to wait.

The picture was supposed to be released in February, but it was not. Instead, there was a small private showing, to which Annie and Helen and Polly were invited. Everyone agreed that the childhood scenes were perfect. But the scenes in which Helen herself appeared needed "strengthening" was the tactful word they used. More pictures were made, in New York, and again Annie and Helen and Polly settled down to wait.

They were still waiting in July, when Helen wrote her mother that the latest news was that the picture would open in a Broadway theater in October.

"That means," she added, "that we shall not receive our payments until then. We have been frightfully hard up, Mother. But we shall manage all right. Our credit is good, and people understand. Everyone believes in the success of the picture."

While they were waiting, Annie and Helen made a trip to Baltimore to visit the blinded soldiers in a military hospital called Evergreen. It was their first experience meeting young men newly blinded in battle, and it was hard on both of them, especially Annie, who could hear and who had some eyesight left. Blind men were everywhere, some of them mere boys, trying to accept the fact that they would have to spend the rest of their lives in darkness.

"Gee, Miss Keller," one of them said to Helen, Annie spelling out his words in her hand, "I read about you in school, but I never thought I'd be blind myself!"

The stupid things that some visitors said about the

soldiers in their hearing—they seemed to think they were deaf as well as blind—infuriated Annie. Such remarks as "I'd rather my son were dead than blind," or, "What will he do when he goes home from here?"

Talking with the soldiers, Helen did not try to paint a rosy picture of the future. It was going to be difficult, she told them, no matter how they looked at it. They would have bad days, when they would feel terribly lonely, cut off from everyone. For such days, there would be only one cure—work. All of them were being taught to do things with their hands, weaving, making baskets, binding books, typing.

"And I can tell you from experience," she would add, "that each triumph brings its compensations."

Years later, during World War II, Helen and Polly would spend months again visiting blind soldiers in military hospitals, both here and abroad. Helen's speech was imperfect, but they understood her, and the inspiration she gave them, the doctors and nurses said, was beyond price.

In July, while they were still waiting for the opening of *Deliverance,* a friend drove Annie and Helen to Boston to see John Macy, who was ill.

"He seemed like a feeble old man," Helen wrote her mother. "Something went wrong with his back, and that, with the heat, knocked him out, as he expressed it. He said he would come to New York as soon as he got back some strength."

Before returning to New York, they drove out to Wrentham. It must have been hard on Annie, although she apparently kept her feelings under control for Helen's sake. For Helen broke down.

"I thought," she wrote her mother, "I could visit the old Wrentham place with some equanimity, but alas! As we came away, I just sobbed aloud, greatly to my own mortification."

Annie and Helen returned to New York to find all the actors out on strike and the theaters dark. It was the beginning of Actors' Equity, the union to which all actors on the so-called legitimate stage now belong. They struck in the summer of 1919 to gain recognition for their newly formed union. Everybody was involved, from the most famous celebrities in show business down to the girls in the chorus lines.

Annie and Helen were naturally on the side of the striking actors, and Helen marched in the picket lines, along with the Barrymores, Ethel and John, Ed Wynne, Marie Dressler and the distinguished baritone, John Charles Thomas.

With all the actors out on strike, the theater owners turned to movies. Motion picture actors were not involved in the strike. And one of the pictures they used was the Helen Keller movie, *Deliverance*. It opened on a wild, stormy night, August 18.

Box seats were sent to Annie, Helen and Polly, but they did not go. Helen publicly stated the reason. The theater owners were using her motion picture as a strikebreaker! If they had gone anywhere that evening, they would have attended a gala performance which was put on by all the big Broadway stars to raise money for their strike fund. But the weather was bad, it was difficult for Polly to manage both Annie and Helen in large crowds, even under more favorable conditions, so they stayed home.

In spite of the weather, *Deliverance* opened to a packed house. The opening-night audience burst into cheers at some of the early scenes, especially the one in which Helen spoke her first words, "I am not dumb now."

When the newspapers came out the following day, the

critics had given the picture what is known in show business as "rave" reviews. *The New York Times* called it a remarkable success, compelling. The *New York World* called it a masterpiece. One critic said it was far more absorbing than a love story. And ads inserted in the theater columns said:

"Strong men were moved to tears, children sat spellbound, women were torn with emotion and all were awakened to a new realization of the possibilities of life."

When Polly read the reviews to Annie, who spelled them into Helen's hand, the three of them hugged each other in delight. *Deliverance* had come through. They would soon be rich. No more financial worries. Complete relaxation, with money for a finer house, a car and chauffeur, beautiful clothes, travel. Money to be put aside for Teacher. Money to buy presents for their friends and to give freely to people who needed it.

Deliverance lasted on Broadway a month, but there was never another packed house. Although Annie and Helen had no way of knowing it, the house that opening night must have been largely "papered," free tickets sent out to people whose influence might count. From then on, *Deliverance* played to steadily diminishing audiences until finally it was taken off and sent out on the road.

It fared no better on the road. The critics may have liked it, as they obviously did. But the public did not. People went to the movies not to be inspired, but to be entertained. And there were plenty of more entertaining movies, with such stars as Norma Talmadge, Mabel Normand, Harold Lloyd, Elsie Ferguson and the most famous "vamp" of all time, Theda Bara.

Financially *Deliverance* was a complete and ignominious flop.

CHAPTER XVIII

BEHIND THE FOOTLIGHTS

A NNIE AND HELEN never received any money from their motion picture beyond the advance, which they spent in Hollywood. But *Deliverance* was not a total loss, for it opened a way for Helen Keller to earn more money than she had ever earned in her life before.

As the weeks lengthened out into months after the Broadway opening, and no money was forthcoming, the plight of the three women in the little house in Forest Hills must have become more desperate than it had ever been before. Not only were they without any income, except for Mr. Carnegie's pension, but they were in debt. And always in the back of Helen's mind was the worry about Teacher's financial insecurity. More lecture tours seemed to be the only way out. But the lecture bureaus were not interested.

One day, when their finances were really at their lowest ebb, a young musician named George Lewis came to see them. Mr. Lewis, a war veteran recently discharged from the army, had written a song about Helen, which he called "Star of Happiness."

Young Mr. Lewis had not only a song, but an idea. He had seen *Deliverance,* had read the reviews after the Broadway opening and thought Helen might do well on the stage. He knew more about vaudeville than he knew about any other branch of show business, and he suggested that she try to get a vaudeville contract.

Vaudeville those days was a very important part of the world of entertainment. There were two big chains, the Orpheum Circuit and Pantages. In nearly every city in the country, even in small cities, both had theaters, with the programs changing every week.

The programs were a kind of combination of the circus and the Chautauqua. There were animal acts, soft-shoe dancers, acrobats, Swiss bell ringers and comedians. Some of the most successful radio and television comedians to-day—Jack Benny, for instance—got their start in vaudeville. People everywhere packed the vaudeville theaters. There were no night clubs to furnish entertainment back in the 1920's.

The Orpheum Circuit, larger and more prosperous of the two chains, had recently introduced a new act. As headliners they were using opera stars, celebrated pianists and violinists and noted speakers, and paying them salaries that compared favorably with those received by motion picture stars. Among the early headliners were the poet Carl Sandburg and Ernestine Schumann-Heink, of the Metropolitan Opera and the concert stage, the most famous contralto of her day. Mr. Lewis thought Helen Keller could fill one of these spots.

Annie and Helen were shocked by the idea—Annie never did get over it—but in their need they told Mr. Lewis to go ahead and see what he could do.

Mr. Lewis knew two successful theatrical agents, Harry

and Herman Weber, brothers. When he approached them with his idea, they were unimpressed.

"Vaudeville is entertainment," one of the brothers reminded him. "People go to laugh and have a good time. What's funny or entertaining about a woman who is blind and deaf? We could never sell an act like that."

But young Mr. Lewis was persistent. He made them read the reviews of *Deliverance*, containing some laudatory comments on Helen as an actress. And he finally persuaded them to go out to Forest Hills to see her.

They said later that what they expected to find was a gloomy household centered on a woman who could not see or hear. They got the surprise of their lives. Far from being pathetic, Helen Keller was a warm, gay, vital human being. She had poise and charm and a sense of humor that could not be obscured even by her imperfect speech. In a kind of daze, they found themselves offering to try to get her a vaudeville contract. After they left, they told themselves that she would either fill the theaters—or empty them. They were taking a chance, and they knew it. But the idea offered a challenge which they could not resist. Harry Weber became Helen's manager.

Before the Webers started trying to sell the act, they warned Annie and Helen that the audiences they would face in vaudeville were apt to be quite different from those they had encountered on lecture tours.

"They'll be made up of plain, ordinary people," Harry Weber told them. "They go to the show to have a good time. Sometimes they can be tough. If they like you, you'll be made. If they don't—well, we might as well ring down the curtain. I think they'll like you. If I didn't, I wouldn't try to sell your act. But I can't offer you any guarantee that they will."

His remarks did nothing to improve the morale of An-

nie and Helen, already jittery over the prospect of going
into vaudeville. But they did appreciate his frankness.
And they went along with him. They had no other place
to go.

With Mr. Lewis, they worked out an act built around
his song "Star of Happiness." The Webers rejected it.
It was too long, they said, and too elaborate.

"We've got to keep it simple," they insisted. "It can't
run over twenty minutes."

When the Webers got through with it, the act was not
unlike the performance Annie and Helen had given on
the lecture platform, only it ran twenty minutes instead
of an hour or an hour and a half. Also it had music—not
Mr. Lewis' song, but Mendelssohn's "Spring Song." And
a great deal of attention was given to the setting.

There were long, careful rehearsals until both Annie
and Helen knew exactly what they were to do every minute while they were on stage. Helen had to know where
and how she was to move. There could be no slip-ups.

The act was tried out on the night of February 16, 1920,
in a small theater in Mount Vernon, a suburb of New
York. The house was sold out. Many customers had to be
turned away at the door.

When the curtain went up, what the audience saw was
a stage set like a handsomely furnished drawing room. On
the right, French windows opened out into a garden. On
the left was a grand piano, on which had been placed a
large, heavy vase filled with flowers. In the background
were elegant velvet hangings.

Annie, wearing a beautiful new evening gown, came on
stage first, a spotlight playing upon her. She walked down
to the footlights, trying not to blink in the gláre which
hurt her eyes cruelly, and made a short speech about
Helen. She told the audience who Helen Keller was—the

Webers insisted that in some vaudeville audiences there might be patrons who had never heard of her, inconceivable though that might seem to Annie. She described Helen's handicaps and told briefly how she had broken through the barrier that had cut her off from the rest of the world and how she had taught her. Then she retired to the rear of the stage while the orchestra played Mendelssohn's "Spring Song."

This was Helen's cue. Polly, standing with her behind the velvet curtains, gave her a nudge, and Helen parted the curtains and walked out onto the stage. Helen, tall, slender and erect, was still an attractive woman at the age of forty. She, too, wore an elegant new evening gown. She looked like anything but a miserable, defeated middle aged woman bereft of sight and hearing.

She stepped out on the stage right beside the grand piano. Resting her hand lightly upon it, she moved along until she came to the big vase. She was a little uncertain the first few times she did it before an audience, but later, to Harry Weber's delight, she became so sure of herself that she would keep time to the music a little as its rhythm reached her through the vibrations beneath her feet.

As Helen reached the vase, Annie stepped forward, and they advanced together to the footlights. Helen made a short speech about what a wonderful place this world could be if only people would work together and try to help one another. She and Annie had worked hard over her speech, and Helen hoped to be able to deliver it without having Annie translate it for her. But it was decided that this would be taking too big a chance. So Annie repeated it after her, sentence by sentence. When she had finished, the audience was invited to ask questions.

This was substantially the act as it was presented to vaudeville audiences for more than two years all over the

United States and in parts of Canada. From time to time, Annie and Helen changed their speeches a little. But the general outline and the setting remained the same.

The audience in Mount Vernon was warm, friendly, enthusiastic. These people knew Helen Keller. She had lectured in Mount Vernon. But the big test was still to come. One week later, on a Monday afternoon, the show opened in the big Palace Theater, on Broadway.

The Palace was the largest and most important vaudeville theater in the country. And a Monday-afternoon audience, viewing a new show, was the toughest. Practically every actor and actress appearing in plays on Broadway would be there, along with the newspaper critics. If this audience rejected an act, it was doomed. Two more frightened women never appeared on the Palace stage than Annie and Helen that Monday afternoon.

The audience at their first performance at the Palace felt tense and uneasy. This audience did not need to be told who Helen Keller was. There were many present who had followed her career for years with interest and admiration. Many had heard her speak before, many had met her and some were her personal friends. They wanted her to make a success in this new venture, they hoped she would, but they were doubtful. It was so different from anything she had ever done before. They listened with respect to Annie's little speech, but she was conscious of their uneasiness.

Helen, not yet sure of herself, shuffled a little, as most blind people do, as she moved along beside the grand piano. But once Annie had touched her arm, her confidence in herself began to come back. As they stood together behind the footlights, she became relaxed, calm, beautifully poised. There was a kind of radiance about her. As she started to speak, in her weird, guttural voice, a great surge of sympathy and admiration swept through the audience. Both Annie and Helen could feel it, and Helen finished her speech, Annie repeating each sentence after her, to great, crashing waves of applause. One of the critics wrote:

"Before she had been on the stage two minutes, Helen Keller had conquered again, and the Monday afternoon audience at the Palace, one of the most critical and cynical in the world, was hers."

Not only was the opening performance a tremendous success, but Helen Keller continued to "pack 'em in," as they say in show business, all the rest of that week and the next. The act was such a hit that it was held over for an extra week, something which did not happen very often at the Palace. After that, Helen, Annie and Polly set out to tour the big Orpheum Circuit, her weekly salary running into four figures.

During the next two years, the act was rated as one of the biggest box-office attractions in vaudeville. One tour lasted forty weeks and took them into practically every state in the Union. You could hardly name a city where they did not appear, and in many of them more than once. And always it was the same.

As Harry Weber put it: "Give her two minutes, and she'll have 'em eating out of her hand."

With Mr. Weber looking after them, there was no comparison between the comfort in which they traveled now with the discomfort they endured on the lecture trips. No more travel all night in day coaches, but drawing rooms and compartments on de luxe passenger trains. Always the best hotels, the best of everything. And instead of one-night stands, they would spend a week in each city, long enough so that Helen no longer had to sit alone, helpless, waiting for Annie or Polly to come to her, but after a couple of days could find her way about in her hotel room.

They had no sooner started on their first trip than yowls of protest rose from a part of the public, outraged that "dear little Helen Keller" was appearing in vaudeville with trained seals, trapeze performers and Sophie Tucker, billed for years as "the last of the red hot mammas." It was all right and proper, that segment of the public thought, for her to lecture for a pittance in concert halls, churches, schools and private homes. But to "make an exhibition of herself" in vaudeville—it was practically criminal.

For all of them Harry Weber had one answer: "Will you pay her what we do?"

The criticism did not bother Helen in the least. She loved vaudeville and everybody in it, including warm, generous Sophie Tucker, who took the trouble to show Polly how to apply stage make-up to the two stars. And even had the criticism hurt her, she would have gone on. For she was doing something she had wanted to do for years, laying aside some money for Annie. To do this she would have withstood any abuse, endured any insult.

It was a less happy experience for Annie. She was fifty-four years old when they started their career in vaudeville. She was not well. In fact, she would never again be really well as long as she lived. Whenever she had to face the spotlight and the footlights, the stabs of pain in her eyes were almost beyond endurance. Gradually, inexorably, Annie was going blind.

She hated the sham, the cheapness, the petty jealousy among some of the performers backstage.

Sometimes discouraged young actors would come to her with their troubles. When they did, she would lecture them in her forthright manner:

"No matter what happens, keep on beginning and failing. Each time you fail, start all over again, and you will grow stronger, until you find that you have accomplished a purpose—not the one you began with perhaps, but one that you will be glad to remember."

Annie Sullivan knew what it meant to try and fail and try again.

CHAPTER XIX

NEW CAREER

As the vaudeville tours continued, and the fund
Helen Keller was building up for her teacher's security grew into a sizable amount, life became more and
more of a burden to Annie.

She derived no satisfaction from the many compliments
she received for her own performance. People told that
her voice was charming, and they would frequently say,
"You always tell the story of Helen as if you were telling
it for the first time."

How good Helen was may be judged from a letter a
fellow vaudevillian, Carl Sandburg, wrote her on April 8,
1922, as her career in show business was drawing to a
close:

"Dear Helen Keller:
"I saw and heard you last night at the Palace and enjoyed it a thousand ways. It was interesting to watch that
audience minute by minute come along till they loved you
big and far. For myself, the surprise was to find you something of a dancer, shifting in easy postures like a good
blooded race horse. I thrilled along with the audience to

your saying you hear applause with your feet registering to vibration of the stage boards. Possibly the finest thing about your performance is that those who see and hear you feel that zest for living. The zest you radiate is more important than any formula about how to live life."

But letters like that were few and far between. Her audiences generally showed their admiration for Helen Keller by their applause and their interest by the questions they asked. Frivolous, sometimes stupid questions annoyed Annie greatly.

The question asked most often was: "Do you shut your eyes when you go to sleep?"

While Annie fumed inside, Helen would always act as though nobody had ever asked her that question before. She would look thoughtful, then smile and reply, "I've never stayed awake long enough to find out."

The vaudeville performances might not have been so irritating to Annie had she still possessed her own zest for living. But she was weary and far from well. She had always been susceptible to colds. They became more and more frequent, and she could not shake them off as she had been able to do when she was younger.

The pain in her eyes from the lights was almost beyond endurance. Eye doctors she consulted in various cities, trying to find some relief, told her she must stop at once. If she did not, they predicted, she would soon become totally blind. Cataracts had begun to form on her eyes.

Helen tried to persuade her to let Polly substitute for her, but Annie stubbornly refused. Helen was doing this for her. She must carry her share of the load. So she went doggedly on, tired, ill, in pain. No one could make her stop.

Finally in Toronto, late in 1921, she had to go to bed

with a severe attack of influenza, and Polly took over temporarily. But as soon as she was able to stand up, Annie returned to the act, trying not to blink at the cruel, stabbing lights.

She gave her last performance one night in January, 1922, in Des Moines, Iowa. A bad cold developed into bronchitis, and she lost her voice completely. From that night on, Polly took her place as long as the trips continued, telling in the third person how Annie Sullivan had led a little girl out of her dark and silent prison cell. Although Helen missed having Teacher at her side, she was relieved.

In the meantime, a large number of organizations devoted to aiding the blind had decided to get together and form a national coordinating agency to act as a clearinghouse for their efforts. In 1921, the American Foundation for the Blind came into existence, with M. C. Migel, of New York, as its president.

Looking about for someone to give prestige to the new organization and at the same time help to raise the money needed for its support, the foundation naturally turned to the most famous blind person in the world, Helen Keller. She was an experienced speaker, and she had been demonstrating for years that she knew how to win the sympathy and admiration of audiences. For some unknown reason, Mr. Migel and his associates were unaware of what Helen Keller was doing at that time. Mr. Migel instructed his secretary to get in touch with her.

Annie and Helen and Polly were at home in Forest Hills between trips when one day the telephone rang. Polly answered it. She told Mr. Migel's secretary that of course Miss Keller would be very much interested in the foundation and would like to help.

"But she can't do anything about it now," Polly added

in her Scottish accent with a burr in it. "She is leaving tomorrow on a vaudeville tour."

The secretary was so shocked that she hung up without saying another word. Helen Keller in vaudeville! Unthinkable! For the time being, the foundation abandoned its idea of using her as a shining symbol.

In the late spring of 1922, Annie, Helen and Polly returned to Forest Hills to a house literally jammed with unanswered mail. They never had been able to catch up with it during the two years they were on the road, and now they must face it—thousands of letters. Letters all over the place, some of them a couple of years old, dusty and smelling of mold. Something had to be done about them. Annie thought they should be answered.

While Polly did the housework (they could probably have hired a maid if Helen and Polly had been willing to dip into Teacher's security fund, but this they steadfastly refused to do), Teacher spent hour after painful hour going through those letters. Those that were important or urgent, Helen answered herself, but someone had to read them to her. Polly worked on them when she could find the time. But the great burden was on Annie.

Hundreds of the letters were from children, many of whom had undoubtedly given up expecting a reply even if they remembered having written in the first place. They were the sort of letters children write to celebrities:

"I am fine. How are you? Are you surprised to get a letter from somebody you don't know? I am nine, going on ten. How old are you? Could you please send me your autograph? We have a Helen Keller club. Could you send us a picture of yourself? How did you happen to be blind and deaf?" And so on.

It hurt Annie not to answer them. She hated to disappoint a child. Friends urged her to throw them away and did manage to destroy several bushels of them without her realizing it. But Annie read all she could, pausing frequently because her eyes could take no more punishment. Since it was impossible to answer all of them immediately, she stuffed them into filing cabinets, desk and bureau drawers, behind the books in bookcases. And in the meantime there was the current mail, always heavy, as it had been ever since Helen was a child.

For two years, from 1922 until 1924, they toiled on, trying to keep up with the mail as it came in and at the same time to clean up the backlog. The only interruptions were brief summer vacations to get away from the heat, scattered vaudeville appearances and speaking engagements. Helen was constantly in demand to address state commissions for the blind and advise them, always with Teacher's help, how to set up their programs and to plead before state legislatures for laws to prevent blindness in children from diseases like trachoma by providing proper medical care and to protect and aid the adult blind.

Finally, in 1924, the American Foundation for the Blind, having recovered from the shock over her appearing in vaudeville, again approached Helen and offered her a position with a steady income that would comfortably support the three women. Helen Keller, aged forty-four, entered upon a career she would follow for the rest of her life. Annie was fifty-eight years old.

The foundation's immediate need was for money, and once more Annie, Helen and Polly took to the road. Their purpose was to raise an endowment fund for the foundation. Helen could have done nothing without Annie and Polly. And without Helen, there would have been no job, no income.

The drive had important support. President Coolidge became its honorary chairman; Henry van Dyke was its active chairman. Among the large contributors were Henry Ford and his son Edsel, John D. Rockefeller, Jr., Joseph Widener, George Eastman and Felix Warburg.

But in their trips around the country, Annie and Helen aroused the interest of thousands of small contributors. Even school children gave their pennies. When they were not on the road, Annie helped Helen draft letters to possible contributors.

Helen's new career was to Annie's liking, although she herself did not enjoy asking people for money, even for someone else. The trips were not unlike the old lecture tours, only they were easier. They would stay two or three days in one locality, schedules were carefully arranged and everything possible was done for their comfort. For a time, Annie seemed much more like her old self.

But her eyesight was slowly, inexorably failing, and by early 1927, at the insistence of her eye doctor and devoted friend, Dr. Conrad E. Berens, of New York, she had given up most of the traveling.

For some time Helen's publishers (Doubleday) had been trying to persuade her to bring her autobiography up-to-date with a new book. Soon after the New Year, 1927, Annie suggested that Helen take a year's leave of absence from the foundation and write the book. Helen reluctantly agreed.

Before she started work on that book, however, a clergyman friend persuaded Helen to write a shorter book, about her religion. She wrote it amid constant complications and interruptions.

In the spring, Polly left for Scotland on a well-earned vacation. Annie and Helen, with their great Dane, Sieglinde, were alone in the house in Forest Hills. Helen did what she could to help with the housework, finding it a welcome relief from long hours at her typewriter. But

Annie had to do the cooking. She managed largely by ear and touch. By listening intently, she could tell when the coffee began to percolate. She could tell when the toast was brown by the heat in it.

Their friends worried about the two of them alone in the house, and it was difficult to reach them. Helen, of course, could not hear the doorbell or the telephone, and half the time Annie did not bother to answer them. With Sieglinde in the house, Annie and Helen did not worry. Sieglinde was as big as a Shetland pony, and the sight of her and the sound of her thunderous bark would send strangers fleeing to the street in terror. Annie and Helen had raised her from puppyhood. With them and with visitors whom she knew, she was as gentle as a kitten. But to possible intruders, Sieglinde could be truly awesome.

Helen finished *My Religion* toward the end of the summer, before Polly's return, and Annie undertook to read the manuscript back to her. Before starting, she belatedly, and briefly, followed the instructions Dr. Berens had implored her to follow, giving her eyes a rest. He had provided her with some eyeglasses with powerful telescopic lenses. The lenses were so thick and so heavy that she could wear them only for short periods. She had not proceeded very far before even the telescopic lenses failed her. Annie could not read a word.

For a time she and Helen sat in stunned silence. Then Annie called Helen's publisher, F. N. Doubleday, for help. His response was quick and generous. He sent a young editorial assistant, Miss Nella Braddy, to the rescue. She read the manuscript to Annie, and Annie spelled it into Helen's hand.

Even before the work on *My Religion* was quite finished, Annie and Miss Braddy started gathering material together for the book the publishers had asked for, the book to bring Helen's autobiography up to date. It was a job before which any researcher would have quailed. They had to drag the material in bits and pieces out of filing cabinets so crammed that it was difficult to open the drawers.

Just as Annie had never kept any day-by-day record during the early stages of Helen's education, she had kept no record of the crowded years since her graduation from Radcliffe. There were no diaries, no scrapbooks, hardly any newspaper clippings. Even copies of the many articles Helen had written for various publications—some important, many small and obscure—were mostly lacking. There was a complete record of only one winter, the winter Annie spent in Puerto Rico. Helen had kept the letters she and Teacher exchanged that winter. Most of the book would have to be dug out of their memories—Annie's, Helen's and Polly's.

Work on the book, which was called *Midstream,* began as soon as the manuscript of *My Religion* was sent off to the publishers. Nella Braddy was assigned to stay on with Annie and Helen until it was finished.

There were countless interruptions. While Helen was on leave of absence, she still owed some obligations to the foundation. She and Annie were always available for advice and help.

Before the book was finished, Sieglinde died of old age, and Helen and Annie were so upset that no work was done for days.

And always there was the mail. Hundreds of letters pouring in as they had for years. Someone had to read them, sort them and see to it that those that were important were answered. Polly returned in the autumn, took over the housework and answered letters whenever she could find the time. Nella Braddy learned the manual alphabet so that she, too, could communicate with Helen, thereby easing somewhat the load on Annie and Polly.

Hour after hour, day in and day out, Annie and Nella Braddy sat together, listening to the clicking of Helen's typewriter as she worked up in her attic study, while Polly busied herself with the housework and answered mail. Two people thrown together as they were either grow to dislike each other, or they become intimate friends. Annie and Nella Braddy became intimate friends.

Spending so many hours together as they did, it was natural that Annie should talk of the past. Nella Braddy was a sympathetic listener, and before the book was finished Annie had told her the whole story of her life, including the wretched childhood years at Tewksbury.

It was the first time Annie had ever told anyone about Tewksbury, unless, when she was much younger, she told it to Dr. Bell's gentle old secretary, Mr. Hitz. There is no record that she did, but once, probably during the early Wrentham days, she and Mr. Hitz made a trip to Feeding Hills, where she was born, and Annie tried to find out what had become of her sister Mary. Apparently she did not find out, although she and Mr. Hitz called on old Bridget Sullivan, widow of her father's brother. Annie did not reveal her identity, and only after she had gone did Bridget become vaguely suspicious.

Naturally Nella Braddy realized that there was a book in the story of Annie Sullivan's life. Amazingly, she finally persuaded Annie to let her write it. For years, Helen had been wanting to write a biography of her teacher, but Annie always put her off, saying, "If you write about your life, you write about mine, too."

Once the decision was made to let Nella Braddy write the book, there was one thing Annie had to do. One afternoon in the autumn of 1930, she sent everybody out of the house in Forest Hills, sat down alone with Helen and painfully spelled into her hand the whole story of Tewksbury, confessing that all the gay, enchanting tales she had told her about her own childhood were untrue.

Helen was fifty years old, Annie sixty-four. For forty-four years Annie Sullivan had kept her secret from the one human being who was closer to her than anyone else on earth.

✖

CHAPTER XX

AUTUMN DUSK

Fᴿᴏᴍ 1929 ᴏɴ, Annie Sullivan made few public appearances, partly at the insistence of Dr. Berens and partly because it had become so difficult for her to move about in unfamiliar surroundings. She was clumsier than Helen Keller was.

That year, Dr. Berens removed a cataract from her right eye, and for a time she could see a little better. But she was as improvident with what was left of her eyesight as she had always been with money.

The printed word had become as important to her as it had been when she was a child at Tewksbury, where Tillie Delaney haltingly read aloud to her anything Annie could find. Helen, Polly and Nella Braddy were forever finding her with her nose in a book and taking it away from her. Friends offered to read aloud to her, and sometimes they did, but it did not satisfy her. To enjoy a book completely, she had to read it herself.

She rebelled fiercely at her failing eyesight and her aging body. Annie Sullivan, who had so magnificently helped Helen Keller to overcome her handicaps, could not help herself.

At times she was unreasonable, bitterly resentful. After such outbursts she would apologize impulsively: "I have behaved like a naughty child and cried for the moon and disobeyed all my own injunctions to treat a handicap as an opportunity for courage."

Annie made one of her rare public appearances when, in 1931, she received an honorary degree from Temple University, in Philadelphia. It was the only honorary degree she ever received, and it took Helen and the university a year to persuade her to accept it.

On December 17, 1930, she dictated to Polly a letter to Charles E. Beury, president of the university, in which she declined to accept the degree and added:

"It is a valuation to which I do not consider my education commensurate. All my life I have suffered in connection with my work from a sense of deficiency of equipment. To take pleasure in such a degree as you so graciously wish to confer upon me I should have to feel I deserved it.

"All the satisfaction that belongs to me—which I derive from the fact that I have discharged my duty toward my beloved pupil Helen Keller not unsuccessfully—I shall realize when she is honored."

Annie and Helen were to have received their honorary degrees together, and Helen, accompanied by Polly, went to Philadelphia to accept hers. A few hours later, Annie and Nella Braddy slipped quietly into Philadelphia and found seats far back in the audience.

After Helen had received her degree, the chairman of the assembly, to Annie's horror, proposed that a degree be conferred on Helen's teacher—"by force if necessary."

He asked everyone who agreed with him to rise. Only Annie, embarrassed and miserable, remained seated.

A year later, only after the university authorities threatened to go to Forest Hills and confer the degree upon her there, Annie gave in and went to Philadelphia and accepted it. But she still thought she should not have done it.

While Annie felt guilty, Helen was happy. From the time she was a girl and realized that she got all the credit for her achievements, while Teacher got all the blame for her mistakes, Helen suffered over the injustice. She deeply resented any slight to her teacher, and there were many of them. There was little she could do to prevent them, however, since Annie invariably hung back when she tried to draw her forward and see that she got recognition.

Although she no longer went on tours for the foundation with Helen and Polly and seldom appeared in public, Annie did a great deal of traveling in the early 1930's, all of it in Europe. There were three trips, in 1930, 1931 and 1932, and they were made partly at the urging of Dr. Berens, who thought the change and relaxation would be good for her.

The objective was always the same, to find some quiet, rural spot in England, France, or Scotland where they would settle down for a restful summer. But it could never be fully achieved. For Helen Keller had not been abroad before, and she was swamped with invitations, honors and requests for speeches. She and Polly tried to spare Annie as much as possible, and they did manage to get in a few carefree weeks in a lovely cottage in Cornwall, in a village in Brittany, in an old farmhouse in the Scottish highlands.

By the end of the summer in 1932, Annie was so worn

out and ill that Helen took a leave of absence from the foundation, and they stayed on in Scotland through the winter. Doctors in Glasgow noted the fact that she was having some heart trouble. She would need a great deal of rest.

When they returned to Forest Hills in the spring of 1933, a solution was found to a problem that had worried Helen deeply. Her work for the foundation required that she and Polly be away from home a great deal, always traveling and making speeches. Leaving Annie alone in the house in Forest Hills was sheer torment for Helen, even though Annie insisted that she was not alone. Three dogs had taken the place of Sieglinde—two terriers and another great Dane.

Finally, when Helen was at her wit's end, a young man named Herbert Haas came to work for them. Annie liked him from the beginning. He was a cheerful young man, with a good sense of humor and a gift for telling stories. He could cook, take care of the house, look after the dogs, drive the car and keep the household accounts straight. He knew how to fix typewriters and Helen's Braille machine when it broke down. Not only did he quickly learn the manual alphabet, but he learned to write in Braille, so he could copy articles Helen wanted to read. And most important of all, he could keep Annie amused by the hour with his droll conversation. Life in the house in Forest Hills was much better after Herbert Haas came.

Although she was far from well, and her eyesight was again deteriorating in spite of all that Dr. Berens could do, Annie still had flashes of her old gayety. She loved to entertain when Helen and Polly were at home, and guests who came were never made aware of Annie's failing health. Always there was good food, witty conversation, two delightful hostesses. Only after they had left would their friends sometimes remember, with a kind of awe, that one of the hostesses was blind and deaf and the other practically blind!

Looking about for some new interest, Annie heard of a neglected blind and deaf baby girl in Kentucky. It took all the persuasive powers of Helen, Dr. Berens and her other friends to keep Annie from adopting the baby and starting all over again with her, as she had with Helen. She was convinced that such a care and responsibility would somehow accomplish a miracle and bring back her old health and vigor. She finally gave in, but not without a struggle, and a home and another teacher were found for the baby girl.

By 1935 Annie's vision was again as bad as it had been before Dr. Berens removed the cataract from her right eye. To her, the obvious thing to do was to have another operation. But this time Dr. Berens shook his head. It would do no good, he said.

Weeping bitterly, Annie put her arms around his neck and pleaded with him to try just once more. He patiently and gently explained to her over and over again that it would not help her, but she refused to listen to him. Finally he reluctantly performed the operation, and, as he had predicted, it failed to help her. Annie Sullivan was as blind as she had been when she was a child at Tewksbury. Reading, which was the very bread of life to her, would never be possible again unless she read Braille.

Helen Keller undertook to teach Annie to read Braille, as Annie had taught it to her when she was a child. Annie had always disliked Braille, and while she had learned again to write in Braille the winter she was in Puerto Rico so that she could write to Helen, she had not read Braille since the first successful operation on her eyes when she was fifteen years old. As hard as Helen tried, Annie was not a good pupil.

"It's not the big things in life that one misses through loss of sight," she told a friend, "but such little things as being able to read. I have no patience, like Helen, for the Braille system because I can't read fast enough.

"Helen is and always has been well balanced, in her blindness as well as in her deafness. But I'm making a futile fight of it, like a bucking broncho."

At times her rebellious spirit would flare up, as of old, and she would be angry and unmanageable. And again, to Helen, she would apologize: "I have wasted time grieving over my eyes. I am very, very sorry, but what is done is done. I have tasted the bitterest drop in my cup."

It was while she was in a hospital, recovering from an operation on her eye, that Annie Sullivan and Alexander Woollcott became friends. Alexander Woollcott those days was probably the most successful, respected—and feared —drama critic, columnist and radio personality in New York. His merciless wit struck terror into the hearts of actors, playwrights and producers.

But there was another side to Alexander Woollcott. He probably met Annie when he went to the hospital to see the movie producer, Samuel Goldwyn, who was a patient in the next room. He discovered that Annie had been sending all the big bouquets and plants she received to Mr. Goldwyn. Since she could not see them, they were of no use to her! So every day Alexander Woollcott would send Annie Sullivan a small, fragrant bouquet, something she could hold in her hand and sniff. Sometimes it would be a gardenia, sometimes a sprig of mignonette, sometimes some rose geranium leaves. And the little bouquets were accompanied by amusing notes.

Annie was shy and embarrassed the first time Alexander

Woollcott came to see her after her return to the house in Forest Hills. He made it very plain that he had come to see her, not Helen. And she could not understand why so successful and worldly a man should be interested in her.

But her shyness wore off after a time in her keen delight at his wit and his humor. He came again and again and presently began reading aloud to her. No one else had ever been so successful at reading aloud to Annie Sullivan. The visits continued for many months. For years, Alexander Woollcott kept on his desk a crystal elephant she had given him for being, as he expressed it "a good boy."

In her restlessness and her rebellion against her blindness and her ill health, Annie often spoke longingly of Puerto Rico, where she had spent the winter when it was thought she had tuberculosis.

"If I could get back there, or to some similar place," she told Helen, "I believe I'd feel better. Puerto Rico did wonders for me that winter."

So in October, 1935, Annie, Helen, Polly and Herbert Haas went to Jamaica. While the others were enchanted with the palms, beautiful flowers, mountains and gaily painted buildings, Annie was too tired to enjoy them, and she could not see them. They cut short their trip and returned to Forest Hills.

It was a busy winter for Helen, and she and Polly were away a great deal. Annie's interest in Helen's job and the work that was being done for the blind remained keen, and when Helen was at home, they talked a great deal about it. Annie regretted that more was not being done for the blind-deaf. But the training of a child who could neither see nor hear required service that was expensive and hard to obtain.

"What a blind-deaf person needs," Annie observed with a sigh, "is not a teacher but another self."

Annie Sullivan had been Helen Keller's "other self" for nearly fifty years.

Helen and Polly gave a birthday party for Annie on April 14, 1936, Annie's seventieth birthday. It was a festive occasion, and old friends heaped a great deal of praise upon Annie Sullivan. Some of it embarrassed her, and she did not take any of it very seriously, except Helen's toast:

"Here's to my teacher, whose birthday was Easter morning in my life."

That spring, Annie made one more effort to pull herself together. She thought a summer away from New York, somewhere in the mountains near a lake, would help her. Polly found a place in the Laurentian Mountains, near Quebec. But the trip was too much for Annie, and it was too cold. She spent most of the summer in bed.

They returned to New York in the early autumn, and, after a brief stay in a hospital, where nothing could be done for her, back to the house in Forest Hills, which Annie would never leave again. Her tired heart was giving out.

For the rest of her life, Helen Keller would carry with her the memory of one lovely evening in October, 1936. Annie was feeling better than usual and was able to sit up in a big armchair in her room. Herbert Haas had been to the rodeo in Madison Square Garden, and his amusing account of the show made Annie chuckle with delight as she spelled his words into Helen's hand.

Not long after that evening, Annie Sullivan dropped into a coma, from which she did not return. She slipped quietly out of this world on October 19, 1936.

Her funeral, in the Park Avenue Presbyterian Church,

was attended by many famous persons. Dr. Harry Emerson Fosdick, pastor of the Rockefellers' church, on Riverside Drive, preached the sermon. Her body was cremated, and a few days later the urn containing her ashes was placed in the National Cathedral, in Washington, D. C., where rest the remains of Woodrow Wilson. It was the first time such an honor was accorded any teacher—or any woman. In the crypt beside the urn, space was reserved to receive some day the ashes of Helen Keller.

In March, 1939, the *Atlantic Monthly* published an article by Alexander Woollcott entitled "In Memoriam: Annie Sullivan." He concluded it with these words:

"At Annie Sullivan's funeral there could have been no one who was not quick with a sense of the unimaginable parting which, after nearly fifty years, had just taken place. While I live I shall remember those services. Not for the great of the land who turned out for that occasion, not for the flowers that filled the church with incomparable incense, nor for the wise and good things which Harry Emerson Fosdick said from the pulpit.

"No, what I shall remember longest was something I witnessed when the services were over, and the procession was filing down the aisle, Helen walking with Polly Thomson at her side. As they passed the pew where I was standing, I saw the tears streaming down Polly's cheeks. And something else I saw. It was a gesture from Helen—a quick flutter of her birdlike hands. She was trying to *comfort* Polly."